I0881552

DAY FIGHTER ACES OF THE LUFTWAFFE 1939–42

CASEMATE | ILLUSTRATED

CASEMATE | ILLUSTRATED

DAY FIGHTER ACES OF THE LUFTWAFFE 1939–42

NEIL PAGE

CASEMATE | ILLUSTRATED

This work could not have been compiled without the generous and unstinting support and encouragement of Jean-Louis Roba, Erik Mombeek, Jean-Yves Lorant, Dr. Jochen Prien, Michel Ledet, Bernd Barbas, Paul Stipdonk and Michael Meyer. Thank you for saying "no problem."

I should like to dedicate this publication to the veterans who took the time to send photos and reminiscences: Ernst Schröder, Hans Weik, Karl-Heinz von den Steinen, Günther Ehrlich, Friedrich-Wilhelm "Timo" Schenk, Jules Meimberg, and Willi Unger. Thank you. All personal accounts translated by Neil Page.

CIS0017

Print Edition: ISBN 978-1-61200-8486
Digital Edition: ISBN 978-1-61200-8493

Design by Battlefield Design
Profiles by Vincent Dhorne
Printed and bound in the Czech Republic by FINIDR, s.r.o.

CASEMATE PUBLISHERS (US)
Telephone (610) 853-9131
Fax (610) 853-9146
Email: casemate@casematepublishers.com
www.casematepublishers.com

CASEMATE PUBLISHERS (UK)
Telephone (01865) 241249
Fax (01865) 794449
Email: casemate-uk@casematepublishers.co.uk
www.casematepublishers.co.uk

Title page: Seen here at Bucharest-Pipera, aircraft of I./JG 28 (temporary designation for III./JG 52) lined up alongside Romanian Bf 109s. A number of German pilots cut short their instructing in late May 1941 to go to Greece but intervened only rarely over Crete.

Contents page: A U.S. four-engine bomber—"*Viermot*"—in the gunsights. Shooting one down was a considerable feat.

Map: Stalingrad, 1942. (German Generalstaff/Library of Congress Geography and Map Division Washington, D.C. 20540-4650)

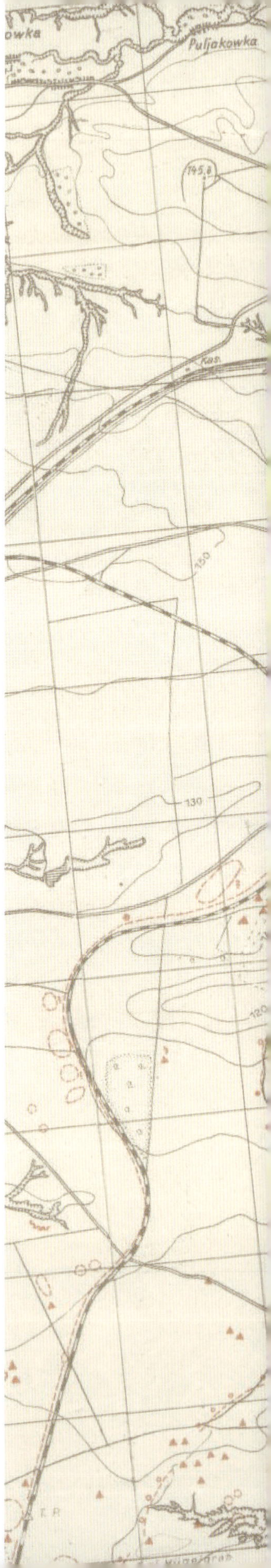

Note: aircraft illustrations and profiles are not to scale.

Note to the reader: Frequently used foreign words, such as unit designations and ranks, and proper nouns are not italicized.

Contents

Timeline of Events

Having been blooded in the Spanish Civil War, by the time of the September 1, 1939 invasion of Poland, the event that triggered World War II, the Luftwaffe had become a force to be feared. While it supported the army during the invasion of the Low Countries and France in May 1940 with great effectiveness, against the RAF in the ensuing Battle of Britain it proved ill-suited to the conduct of a strategic campaign. However in 1941/42, with the invasion of the USSR, and the North Africa/Mediterranean campaigns in full swing, the Jagdflieger—the fighter pilots—achieved some staggering successes and the "high-scoring" aces were widely feted by the propaganda services of the Reich. But as 1942 drew to a close, the tide of war was already beginning to change in dramatic fashion.

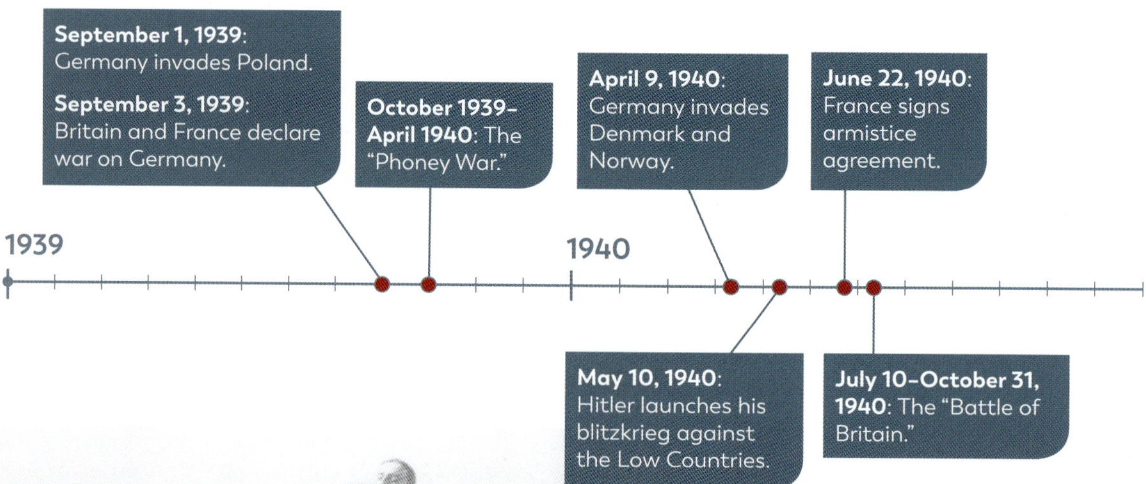

During 1942 Hermann Graf cemented his status as one of the Luftwaffe's greatest aces. In October he returned his 200th *Luftsieg* over Stalingrad, coinciding with the Luftwaffe's high point of the war. Barely three months later, the German 6th Army surrendered.

Hermann Göring laying a wreath at the tomb of the "Red Baron," Manfred von Richthofen.

1941

- **February 1941**: The Afrika Korps is deployed to North Africa.
- **April 6–June 1941**: Germany invades the Balkans and Greece.
- **June 22, 1941**: Operation *Barbarossa:* the invasion of the USSR.
- **December 6, 1941**: Soviet counteroffensive routs German forces at Moscow.

1942

- **June 2, 1942**: Operation *Störfang* opens against the Crimean port of Sevastopol.
  June 21, 1942: Rommel captures Tobruk
- **September 1942**: German troops penetrate deep into the Caucasus and arrive at the Volga.
- **October 23, 1942**: Battle of El Alamein.
- **November 23, 1942**: Soviet offensive traps German 6th Army in Stalingrad.

Robert Ritter von Greim commanded Royal Bavarian Jagdstaffel ("Jasta") 34 from June 1917. He returned some 27 victories and was awarded the Pour le Mérite ("Blue Max"). Here he is seen in front of his Jasta 34 Albatros fighter.

Introduction

The idea that, as soon as he came to power in 1933, Adolf Hitler somehow created a military aviation arm from scratch is one of those myths that has grown up around the Luftwaffe. The Luftwaffe was the synthesis of trial and error in various guises from 1918.

November 11, 1918: Allied victory over the Central Powers. The victors set about imposing harsh peace terms aimed at permanently subduing the defeated Germans. In addition to reparations that were payable until 1988, Germany was restricted to an army of 100,000 and all military aviation was banned. A period of unrest then began across the Rhine, which would see armed conflict, famine, colossal currency devaluation, territorial occupations, social unrest, and street fighting, all culminating in the economic crisis of 1929/33 and Hitler's 1933 *Machtergreifung*—seizure of power.

The closing down of aircraft and manufacturing companies obviously depressed an already bleak economic picture. The aviators themselves—more often than not young men who had not had the chance to complete a course in higher education because of the war—lived from hand to mouth. Perhaps the most renowned of these was future Reichsmarschall Hermann Göring, who had succeeded his comrade Manfred Freiherr von Richthofen at the head of JG 1 in 1918.

Hitler actively sought out support from former Great War veterans, of whom Göring was without question the most famous. On January 30, 1933, Hitler appointed him to head up the brand-new Ministry of Air (RLM or Reichsluftfahrtministerium). Faced with rapid expansion, the recruitment policy was simple: the Reichsmarschall called on fellow veterans of the Great War to help build the new Luftwaffe. Notable aces taking up key positions included Ernst Udet (Generalluftzeugmeister) and Karl Bodenschatz (General der Flieger) appointed to head up Göring's ministerial office in 1933 before being named Luftwaffe Air Attaché at the Chancellery two years later. Former Fokker triplane ace and Jasta 34 commander Robert Ritter von Greim was appointed Kommandeur of the first fighter Gruppe of the new Luftwaffe, I./JG 132.

In 1935/36, the Luftwaffe came out of limbo. A massive construction program was set in motion, with 121 airfields created prior to October 1936.

On July 17, 1936, a group of Spanish generals launched a *Pronunciamiento* (military coup) against the left-wing government, sparking the civil war. Both sides sought international support. On July 25, Hitler was thus forced to receive representatives of General Francisco Franco in Bayreuth during the Wagnerian festival. He was asked to urgently send planes to transport Franco's African army. At first glance, the Führer was cool on the prospect of intervention: the factions were politically foreign "Catholic reactionaries." Secondly, his Luftwaffe was still expanding and could not be weakened; moreover, he did not want to alienate the Western powers. The Reich Chancellor finally and reluctantly acquiesced, convinced by his advisers that, politically, he could not risk Spain falling into communist hands; economically, a Spanish ally would make it possible to obtain raw materials that the Reich desperately needed; and militarily, Air Marshal Göring pushed to test the basics of his Luftwaffe—bombers, transports, fighters, recce machines—in a limited conflict. A veteran of the Great War, he knew that the best military crucible was a war.

Ernst Udet, the second highest-scoring German ace of the Great War, seen at the controls of one of his own Udet U12 Flamingo aerobatic sport biplanes during the early 1920s.

The first fighters dispatched to Spain were Heinkel 51 biplanes, the best fighter in service in the Luftwaffe at the time. However, the He 51s proved inferior to the Soviet I-15 and I-16 fighters in combat and it was quickly evident that the type was obsolete.

Twenty Ju 52 trimotor transports were thus dispatched to Spanish Morocco to organize the airlift of Franco's army. Shortly afterwards a fighter Staffel, comprising six He 51 biplanes, deployed on July 31 to the nationalist sector.

The small German expeditionary air force soon found itself having to actively engage: ordnance was loaded into transport aircraft to fly ad-hoc bombing missions and fighter pilots sought permission to carry out free-hunt sorties. On August 25, Eberhardt and Trautloft each shot down a Breguet 19. Two more suffered the same fate the next day: these were the first victories of the German fighter arm as reconstituted by the Third Reich. On September 6, Oberleutnantes Eberhardt and Knüppel each claimed a Potez, their fifth victories, becoming *Experten*, or aces, but the first air battles with Soviet fighters provided a rude awakening.

As the conflict bogged down, Hitler had to face facts: he had become caught up in the conflict and if the Nationalists wanted to win this civil war, they would need structured German aid. Admiral Wilhelm Canaris therefore met Franco, to offer him increased German aid, independent of the Nationalist forces. The cost of operations would be offset by economic contracts favorable to the Reich. The future Caudillo had little option but to accept, and the Condor Legion was born.

On April 6, 1937, northwest of Ochandiano during the first Nationalist offensive, Günther Lützow downed an I-15—the first enemy aircraft shot down by a Messerschmitt 109. In the space of four months (April–August 1937), Lützow became an ace. To counter the Bf 109, the Soviets engaged the I-16 but successive versions of the Bf 109 (Dora and Emil) arrived in theater in time and air superiority remained the prerogative of the Legion.

Probably the most successful day for J/88 came on February 7, 1938 when no fewer than ten SB-2s and two I-16s were destroyed in a large air battle over the Alfambra. Identifying a weak stretch of the Republican line north of Teruel, Franco had launched a counteroffensive in this area—a flanking attack with a spectacular cavalry charge that helped turn the tide, trapping the Republicans in Teruel.

Hauptmann Walter Grabmann (seven victories in Spain), the last commander of J/88. Appointed Kommodore of ZG 76 in 1940, he was shot down and captured during the battle of France. He subsequently led this heavy fighter Geschwader in operations over England and on September 2, 1940 claimed two Spitfires shot down. He was awarded the Knight's Cross and ended the war in command positions.

On March 31, 1939, the Nationalist victory was complete. The Condor Legion returned to the Reich. German fighters claimed some 314 victories in Spain (the last one on March 6, 1939 was Oberleutnant Hubertus von Bonin's fourth). One hundred and twenty Luftwaffe fighter pilots served in Spain; 34 of them died there (including three due to accidents and five due to illness). There were relatively few aces and certainly none that achieved victory totals like the 40 returned by Nationalist ace Garcia Morato. Ultimately the Germans were "warrior tourists" who came to the country, not to defend their homeland, but to gain combat experience.

Their experiences in the Condor Legion would remain very much a defining characteristic of the group of fighter pilots that shared them. According to some estimates as many as 50 percent of *Jagdflieger* in 1939 had some flying experience in Spain. The "Spaniards" were virtually a breed apart within the Luftwaffe. Their victories in Spain were always counted separately from those won in World War II. An imposing parade took place in Berlin on June 6, 1939 to honor their achievements. Three months later, Germany invaded Poland.

Hermann Göring decorating members of the Condor Legion, Döberitz, June 5, 1939. Second right is Rolf Pingel, an ace with six victories. Pingel was Kommandeur of I./JG 26 during the Battle of Britain.

In Profile:
The Day Fighter Units

Kapitän Lt. Erich Hartmann of 9./JG 52 seen alongside his Bf 109 G-6 Yellow 1 during late 1943. His rudder scoreboard displays 121 victory markings, the highest "score" seen on any of Hartmann's machines. His victims were almost exclusively Soviet fighters. He claimed only 15 of the heavily-armored, low-flying IL-2 Shturmovik ground attack aircraft, far fewer than other top-scoring Eastern Front aces. His chief tactic in combat involved catching lone Soviet aircraft unawares, approaching them from the rear in a shallow dive before zoom-climbing for altitude, avoiding a "dogfight" where possible. Hartmann's supposed 352 victory tally making him the leading fighter ace of WWII has undergone much recent scrutiny.

JG 1 was first formed in May 1939 in eastern Prussia. I./JG 1 was one of the original Gruppen established by the Luftwaffe as part of its pre-war expansion plans. Absorbed into a "new" Geschwader, which would fight mainly in the Netherlands, northern Germany, and Denmark, the new JG 1, established in late 1940 under Oberstleutnant Carl-August Schumacher, was tasked with providing air cover over a large portion of the North Sea coastline, its operational area stretching from the Netherlands to southern Norway. On January 5, 1942, Schumacher handed over command to Major Erich von Selle. JG 1 was one of the primary units opposing the incursions of the "Mighty Eighth"—U.S. Eighth Air Force—from mid-1943. Active in the defense of the Reich (RVT) and then in Normandy, JG 1 adopted the honor title "Oesau" in May 1944 after Kommodore Oesau was killed in action. JG 1 ended the war training on the Heinkel He 162 jet.

JG 2, the oldest JG, named Richthofen, was not too active in 1939, but fought in the West in 1940, then based until early 1944 on the English Channel, before shifting back to Germany and the defense of the Reich. A Gruppe went to North Africa.

JG 3 fought in the West in 1940 and was very active in the USSR where the vast majority of some 6,500 victories were returned by aces such as Wilcke, Kirschner, Gollob, and Dahl. Adopted the honor title "Udet" at the end of 1941. II. Gruppe was engaged in the Mediterranean. Established in late 1943, IV. Gruppe became specialist *Sturmjäger* (bomber destroyers) during April 1944 under Hptm. Wilhelm Moritz. Ended the war in the defense of the Reich (RVT).

JG 4 I. Gruppe was established in 1943 to defend the Romanian oilfields before its transfer to Italy in 1944. Two more Gruppen were subsequently established to serve in the defense of the Reich, including II.(Sturm)/JG 4. In early 1945 I. Gruppe was disbanded while the fighters of II. and III. Gruppen flew ground attack in the East against the Oder bridgeheads with SD 2 fragmentation bombs.

JG 5 was formed mainly in 1941 to operate in the Norway/Finland sector, hence its nickname "Eismeer" (Arctic Ocean). I and II. Gruppe went to France to repulse the Allied invasion in June 1944 and then served in Germany in the RVT.

JG 6 was formed mid-1944 and engaged in the RVT.

JG 7 was formed at the end of 1944 with Me 262 jet fighters.

JG 11 was established in 1943 by splitting JG 1 to reinforce the defense of the Reich.

JG 26 was formed before the war with the honorary name of "Schlageter." Not very active in 1939 but fought vigorously in the West before deploying to the Channel front until 1944 with JG 2. I./JG 26 spent five months in Russia during the first half of 1943. Ended the war in RVT.

JG 27 trained before the war. Fought in 1939/40 in the West before deploying to the USSR and then to Africa. Fought principally in the Mediterranean before ending the war in RVT.

JG 51 campaigned in the West during 1939/40 and thereafter mainly in the USSR. Some elements were engaged in Africa. The end of the war saw JG 51 fighting in the defense of the Reich.

JG 52 was generally considered the most successful of the fighter Geschwader. Fought in the West during 1939/40 before being fully deployed in Russia.

JG 53, the "Pik As," adopted the ace of spades emblem. Actively fought in 1939/40 before leaving for the USSR and then the Mediterranean. From late 1944, it was engaged in RVT.

JG 54 adopted Trautloft's "Grünherz" (green hearts) emblem. Fought in 1940 then mainly in the USSR during the 18-month-long blockade of Leningrad. III. Gruppe was deployed to the West in 1943 and stayed to reinforce the RVT.

JG 76 was created in 1938 with many Austrian pilots. An early luminary of I./JG 76 was Hans Phillip who returned his first kill on September 5, 1939. JG 76 flew operations through the Polish campaign and the battle of France and claimed some 69 Allied aircraft downed, with Lt. Roloff von Aspern (8), Lt. Hans Philipp and Ofw. Max Stotz (both 7) and Oblt. Dietrich Hrabak (6) the top scorers. Disbanded in 1940 but reformed in mid-1944 for the RVT.

JG 77 fought in late 1939 over the German Bight and in the West. I. Gruppe fought on the Channel coast from late August 1940 in the Battle of Britain. Sent to the USSR until 1942 and then to the Mediterranean. In 1943, adopted the "Herz As" (red heart) emblem in honor of fallen Kommodore Müncheberg. In 1944, III. Gruppe of JG 77 was tasked with defending the Romanian oilfields from massive U.S. Fifteenth Air Force incursions. Fought in the West from late 1944 and in the East.

JG 300/301/302 were established as "unguided" single-engine night fighter units in later 1943 after German defenses were blinded by "Window" (chaff) during the Hamburg raids. Pilots were former bomber and instrument-trained "blind flyers." As the Luftwaffe fighter force were not instrument-trained, Gruppen of JG 300 and JG 301 joined the day fighter defenses of the Reich from December 1943 to oppose bombing raids in poor visibility. II. Gruppe JG 300 became a *Sturm* unit in July 1944, by which time the entire Geschwader flew principally daytime sorties countering bomber incursions over the Reich, dedicated Staffeln also flying at night, including the specialist Mosquito hunters of 10./JG 300. In January 1945 JG 300 was transferred to the East, carrying out strafing attacks on Soviet columns before opposing the *Varsity* Rhine crossings in late March.

A JGr. 102 Bf 109 D displaying the Gruppe emblem below the cockpit.

The Polish Campaign and the Phoney War

On September 1, 1939, Germany invaded Poland—an attempt to resolve by force the various territorial and political conflicts that existed between the two nations. Two days later, Great Britain issued an ultimatum, which was ignored. Britain declared war on the Third Reich and once again pushed France to follow its example so that Germany would have to fight, temporarily, on two fronts.

The Western Allies watched as the Polish army were neutralized in just three weeks in what would be dubbed the *Blitzkrieg* or "lightning war." In addition to a fleet of bombers, the Luftwaffe committed nine Jagdgruppen equipped with Bf 109s over Poland. Four of these Gruppen saw no combat, but flew patrols and escorts. This proved particularly frustrating for I./JG 1, two of whose Staffelkapitäne, Balthasar and Adolph, were experienced Ju 88 pilots. The Polish air arm, composed mainly of obsolete PZLs, was swept from the sky in record time. The Bf 109 units were equipped with Jumo-engined D models—virtually obsolescent themselves, although far superior to anything in the Polish inventory. In the end 37 pilots secured some 52 aerial victories between them. I./JG 21 opened the scoring on 1 September when four of its pilots accounted for four PZL 24s. Among the successful aviators was one particular future notable *Experte* (ace), Leutnant Gustav Rödel. I./LG 2 returned eight victories throughout the campaign, including the first "official" victory returned by Hauptmann Harro Harder following his 11 achieved over Spain. Unteroffizier Fritz

Geisshardt and Feldwebel Erwin Clausen opened their scorecards. While I./JG 77 only won three victories, one of these was the first since 1937, attributed to Kapitän Hannes Trautloft. I./JG 76, a fighter Gruppe with a large number of Austrian pilots who had "become" German following the Anschluss of 1938, returned six victories.

However, the leading unit over Poland was I./ZG 2 (which, like II./ZG 1, still flew Bf 109s, specifically in the subordinated JGr. 102), 15 of its pilots being credited with a total of 29 victories. Hptm. Johannes Gentzen, Gruppenkommandeur, claimed no fewer than seven of them from September 2 to 14. Gentzen's Gruppe also claimed some 50 aircraft destroyed on the ground—I./ZG 2 was attached administratively to the Stab/LG 2 and following the progression of Army Group South was in almost constant contact with the Polish Air Force. Unsurprisingly, Gentzen soon became the darling of German propaganda and his exploits featured in books and magazines. On the second day of the offensive, September 2, Gentzen achieved his first victory, downing a PZL P-23 south of Radomsko. War reporter Karl-Georg von Stackelberg recorded events in his 1940 account *Jagdflieger Gruppe G: Jäger an Polens Himmel* (*Fighters in Polish Skies*):

> As soon as our formation sighted the enemy the Hauptmann maneuvered his fighter over the Polish bomber like a hawk over its prey. A burst of fire is unleashed from the MGs. The Polish machine tumbles down and crashes in flames. This is the first "kill." The first white victory marking is carefully painted on the rudder. While the Kommandeur quenches his thirst with his *Waffenwart* and *Bordmechaniker*—the indispensable armorer and mechanic—1. Staffel led by Oblt. Waldemar von Roon gets airborne on another sortie—a free hunt in the vicinity of Lodz.

On September 13 (according to Stackelberg's account) a recce He 111 of KG 55 appeared over the airfield at Debica and, dropping a message, announced that a concentration of Polish machines had been located at Brody, 60 kilometers from the Russian border. Airborne immediately at 15:20 with six machines of 1. Staffel, Gentzen arrived in the vicinity of Brody, overflying the Polish airfield at Hutniki—more or less concealed by woods—before encountering a formation of PZL.23 Karaś on a transfer flight south of Brody:

> at the controls of his machine the Hauptmann glances left, banking his 109 over onto its wing … brown-colored shapes slipping over the treetops—one, two, three … eight Polish combat aircraft. *Hinterdrein!* In behind them! The Poles appear not to have noticed as the Kommandeur gives chase and comes in on their tails. Strapped tight into his 109 he closes on the group and lines up the "tail-end Charlie" in the gunsight, his finger on the firing button. Aiming obliquely, the MGs start to hammer out, followed by the cannon. The Polish machine is hit, somersaults, smashes into the forest. Now for the next one! At treetop height the hunt continues. The Kommandeur unleashes more bursts of fire—the second one is finished off. The other Poles have seen nothing of the fighter that is hot on their heels. The Kommandeur downs the third, then the fourth, all this happens in just seconds … *ein Blitzangriff*—a lightning attack. It is all over in minutes … eight *Abschüsse* in the air and several aircraft shot up on the ground.

In total the pilots of I./ZG 2 claimed 14 Polish machines destroyed. Gentzen was credited with four confirmed victories. One Bf 109 D was lost in the engagement—White 4 flown by Uffz. Wolfgang Koch. On September 15, with the campaign in Poland not yet over, Göring flew into Gerlitz to decorate Gentzen with the Iron Cross 2nd Class.

JGr. 102's Maj. Gentzen receiving the Iron Cross from Göring toward the end of the Polish campaign.

Seen here on patrol over Poland, this may be the Bf 109 Dora usually flown by Oblt. Balthasar, Staffelkapitän 1./JG 1.

A line-up of JG 1 machines somewhere in East Prussia just prior to the launch of the invasion of Poland.

Hptm. Hannes Trautloft claimed his first aerial victory during the invasion of Poland and was appointed Kommandeur of I./JG 20 which later became III. Gruppe of Jagdgeschwader 51.

A line-up of 1./JG 20 machines. Based principally in Döberitz during late 1939, the Gruppe was tasked with the defense of central German airspace before shifting to the western border during early 1940. Successful Spain veteran Oblt. Walter Oesau was the first Staffelkapitän of 1./JG 20. The Staffel "bow and arrow" ("*Pfeil und Bogen*") emblem can be seen on the engine cowlings.

Bf 109 E assigned to Oblt. Walter Oesau, Staffelkapitän of 1./JG 20. It was planned to incorporate the Gruppe into JG 2 but ultimately it was redesignated III./JG 51 during 1940, Oesau being appointed Kapitän of 7./JG 51.

A I./JG 76 Emil shot down during the *Polenfeldzug*, the Polish campaign—note the "Lion of Aspern" emblem. I./JG 76 became II./JG 54 in July 1940.

During this campaign, Adolf Galland was appointed to command a ground support unit, a posting that apparently caused him much consternation.

On October 1, 1939, Warsaw fell. After a short rest, German fighter units returned to the West. On the Western Front, entrenched behind the Westwall (the "Siegfried Line" to the Allies), the German army, reduced to the bare minimum, feared an attack by the combined Franco-British armies. But these were no more effective than during the "Munich Crisis" the previous year. The establishment of a joint command would take months. Poland's "pseudo-defenders"—who were careful not to declare war on Poland's Soviet aggressor—took no action.

Elsewhere, RAF Blenheims and Wellingtons had raided the German naval bases of Wilhelmshaven and Brunsbüttel on September 4, 1939. Airborne from Nordholz, Fw. Alfred Held and Fw. Hans Troitzsch of II./JG 77 downed two medium twins for the first victories returned by the Geschwader, these also becoming the first RAF aircraft to fall to the guns of Luftwaffe fighters. In a widely circulated newspaper account Held recalled:

A favorite of the German propaganda services, Alfred Held of JG 77 had his career rapidly snuffed out by an accident.

> I sighted a twin-engine machine coming under anti-aircraft fire over the Jade Bight [German North Sea coast]. Closing on him I unleashed a burst of fire and huge flames erupted from the left side of the bomber. I couldn't believe what I was seeing—the end already for the British machine. He appeared to be out of control. I gave him another burst and he went straight down and plunged into the sea.

Held did not enjoy his newfound celebrity status for long: he perished in a crash exactly a fortnight later.

On the border with France, JG 53's two Gruppen bore virtually alone the burden of aerial engagements in and around the Saarland throughout September. All six of the Staffeln of JG 53 were led by "Spanish" veterans. The first dogfights with French Curtiss fighters took place on the 8th. In this engagement, Werner Mölders, leading I./JG 53, was shot down and slightly wounded. Mölders likely underestimated the Curtiss's maneuverability and speed, probably based on his battles over Spain.

The next day, a Rotte of 1./JG 53 shot down a Bloch MB.131, Ofw. Walter Grimmling subsequently receiving the first Iron Cross 2nd Class awarded in JG 53 but this Spain veteran would barely survive his victim: he was shot down that afternoon over the Saar.

Border engagements of this type took place every two or three days, with German fighter pilots benefiting from two advantages: 1) the superiority in combat of their Messerschmitt Bf 109s, and 2) the obsolescence of many French aircraft (Les Mureaux, Bloch, etc.).

Like the Poles before them in September 1939 the Armée de l'air's entire fleet of aircraft was essentially outdated, including its most modern fighter, the M.S.406. In an effort to make up the shortfall, the French had placed large orders for foreign types. Most significant of

II./JG 3 Emil wearing the dark green splinter finish displaying the short-lived Sudeten Deutscher Party emblem under the cockpit. The Sudeten German Party had been a major pro-Nazi force in Czechoslovakia prior to the German occupation.

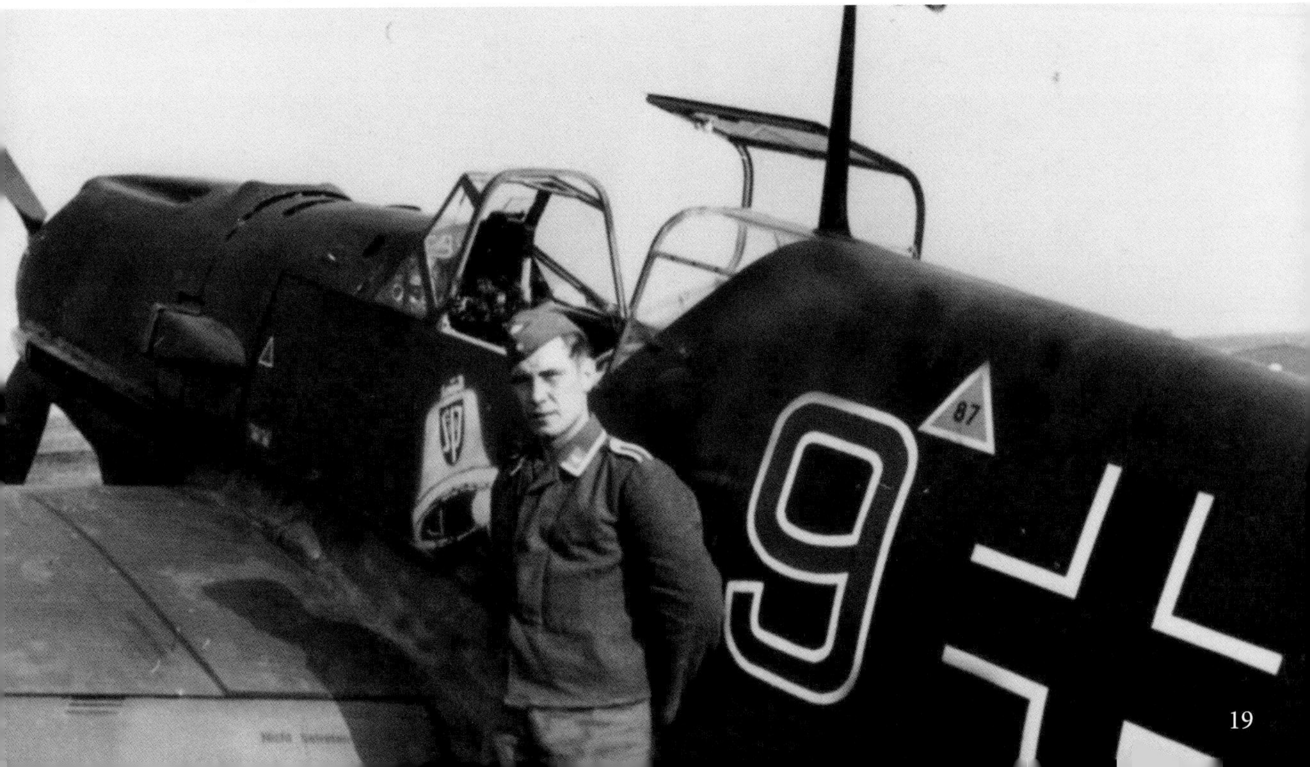

Oblt. Reinhard Seiler was appointed Staffelkapitän of 1./JG 54 on the establishment of this unit, September 13, 1939. His White 7 displayed the Staffel emblem—a chimney sweep carrying a ladder—along with the "top hat" of a Condor Legion JGr. 88 veteran.

these was the American Curtiss P-36 Hawk (Model 75). The French pilots were enthusiastic about the American fighter: here was a relatively fast, maneuverable machine that did not leak oil or hydraulic fluid, whose cockpit was comfortable and well-appointed and whose brakes worked! Many converted immediately from the elderly prewar open-cockpit Dewoitine monoplane fighter.

Luftwaffe pilots claimed some 65 victories in September: on the 10th, Hptm. Rolf Pingel recorded his first "official" victory. On the 20th, Stabsfeldwebel Ignatz Prestele (four victories in Spain) set alight one of the three French balloons destroyed that day, a second being shot down by another "Spaniard," Oblt. Heinz Bretnütz (two victories in Spain). At the end of the morning, Obfw. Willibald Hien (four victories in Spain) was credited with a recce type—a Les Mureaux 115. On the same day, II./JG 53 claimed two victories over Fairey Battles, RAF light bombers operating with the AASF (Advanced Air Strike Force).

On October 6, LeO 451 (No. 6) was the first modern French bomber to be downed by a German fighter.

Also on the 20th, Mölders recorded his first "official" success, downing a French Curtiss. Six days later, the "great ace" of Spain was temporarily withdrawn from the front to create a new III. Gruppe of JG 53 from scratch, where he was subsequently able to fully develop his tactics training young recruits.

September 30 saw a series of bloody aerial battles involving JG 53. In the morning, a formation of five RAF Battles was shot down and, following this bloodletting, the British Expeditionary Force (BEF) command prohibited their dispatch unescorted to the Reich. A series of fights in the afternoon saw more victories but there were two losses, including Obfw. Hien, himself a victor ten days earlier.

The return to the West of the units committed against Poland was particularly welcome. During October the German fighter pilots returned just 12 victories. The Allied air forces, having assessed the quality of their opposition, now only committed forces sparingly. For the first time claims from units returning from the East (such as I./JG 1 and I./JG 77) appeared.

On October 6, Lt. Hans Berthel (2./JG 52) shot down a modern French LeO 451 bomber from GB I/31. On the 30th, in the north, Fw. Erwin Sawallisch (4./JG 77) destroyed a Blenheim west of Heligoland, the former Spanish veteran's first official victory.

On 30 October, Mölders was involved in the first engagement of the recently established III./JG 53. A Blenheim was hit by the new Kommandeur for his second victory in the West and the first for the Gruppe.

A probable re-enactment for the propaganda cameras—a briefing for pilots of 4./JG 77, the Staffel furnishing fighter cover over the German Bight. From left: Oblt. Helmut Henz (Kapitän), Maj. Harry von Bülow-Bothkamp (Kommandeur II./JG 77), Fw. Erwin Sawallisch, and Lt. Heinz Demes. Only von Bülow survived the war.

In November, 20 pilots shared 23 victories. The Allies continue to exercise caution, especially since the weather was not very favorable. On November 6, 1939, one of the most "celebrated" encounters of the Phoney War took place—three flights of GC II/5 P-36 Curtiss Hawks ran into 27 Messerschmitt Bf 109 D (Dora) fighters of JGr. 102 over the Saarland. The highly maneuverable Curtiss fighters secured a number of victories without loss, duly feted in the French media as the battle of "the 9 vs. the 27." The Doras were led in the air by Maj. Gentzen, still the leading Luftwaffe fighter ace. Even though the next day Gentzen claimed an eighth victory, he was recalled to Berlin to be given a dressing down. His unit was then withdrawn from the front and early in 1940 was re-equipped with the Bf 110. At that time the Luftwaffe was still introducing the Emil variant of the Bf 109 (1,000–1,100-hp engine with the advantage of fuel injection), which was clearly better in the air than the Bf 109 D that remained in widespread service in late 1939 and early 1940. The French equivalent of the 109 was the Dewoitine D.520 but when it finally came into service—like most new French aircraft being introduced into service during early 1940—it suffered considerable teething problems.

November 22 was of significance since a first victory (over a French fighter) was claimed by Lt. Helmut Wick (3./JG 2) who would soon become one of the leading fighter pilots of the Luftwaffe. In a newspaper account Wick recalled how:

> fourteen Curtiss fell on us with the advantage of height and the sun at their backs. I quickly had four of them on my tail, but luckily none of them was able to hit me as I twisted and turned and then pulled up into a tight climbing turn. I was soon in a position to open up and lined up the last machine in their formation in the sight. I let him have a short burst. The Curtiss appeared to break up before my eyes, the wings buckling and tearing away.

Also on November 22 and south of Saarbrücken, Hptm. Dr. Erich Mix of the Stab I./JG 53, at 41 probably the oldest fighter pilot in the Luftwaffe, claimed two M.S.406 fighters downed.

On the 23rd, two 1./JG 51 pilots operating over Saarbrücken claimed two Moranes, the first victories for Lts. Hermann-Friedrich Joppien and Friedrich Eberle.

Uffz. Eduard Koslowski of 9./JG 53 returned his first victory shooting down a Les Mureaux 115 on November 6. Here his Yellow 10 in the III./JG 53 segmented camo finish is seen after a forced landing.

Hptm. Werner Mölders, Kommandeur of the recently established III./JG 53 seen in the cockpit of his "*Winkel Dreieck*" ("Chevron Triangle").

JGr. 102 suffered heavy losses in November 1939 shortly after its notable successes over Poland. On the left is Gentzen's "White Chevron Triangle." Note the white victory markings on the tailfin. Nearest the camera is a Bf 109 D-1 of 1. Staffel—both Gruppe and Staffel emblems are visible on the original print.

Seen here on the right, reservist Dr. Erich Mix, mayor of Wiesbaden and Great War aviator, returned to duty in 1939 with the Stab I./JG 53.

Oblt. Wilfried Pufahl's Chevron 3, a Bf 109 E-3 of the Gruppenstab of II./JG 53 seen just prior to the start of the French campaign. Pufahl returned his first victory on the opening day of *Barbarossa*, the invasion of the Soviet Union.

In December, given the bad weather, there were only four victories in the Colmar/Metz sector. But during the month, the RAF launched two major bombing missions targeting Kriegsmarine ships in the north of the Reich. The RAF thus committed unescorted bomber formations based on Giulio Douhet's dubious theories that given the weight of their defensive firepower the bomber would always get through. On December 14, no fewer than ten Wellingtons were claimed by 4. and 5./JG 77 (six losses admitted by the British). This setback apparently failed to deter Bomber Command, the RAF attributing this failure to bad weather.

There was still little understanding that bombers sent so far from their bases and without fighter protection were "birds for the cat." This led to the events of December 18, 1939. On the morning of the 18th *The Times* newspaper had headlined "Graf Spee scuttled without a fight." Now the RAF prepared to send its Wellington bombers, a type that was believed quite capable of defending itself from fighter attack, on the first major air raid of the war—a strike against the capital ships of the Kriegsmarine lying at anchor in Wilhelmshaven. Around midday some 24 Wellingtons (9, 37, 38, and 149 Squadrons) droned across the North Sea. Heligoland Island passed below their starboard wings. The bombers then headed for the Bay of Germany where the alert had already been sounded. II./JG 77 and 11./JG 26 were airborne to intercept the bombers off the Frisian Isles. The carnage soon got underway: the defending fighters "fell on the pride of the RAF like a ton of bricks." By the end of the clash the pilots of II./JG 77 had claimed no fewer than 17 Wellingtons (13 officially confirmed). At this stage of the war RAF bombers did not as yet have self-sealing tanks and were quickly turned into flying torches. Four Bf 109s of II./JG 77 were seriously damaged by defensive fire and a German fighter disappeared with its pilot north of Wangerooge. Winfried Schmidt was credited with his first victory:

> The engagement was coming to an end when I managed to place my Messerschmitt 109 "Kölle Allaf" in a firing position behind one of the fleeing bombers. You learn

Lt. Winfried Schmidt of 5./JG 77 shot down an RAF Wellington on December 18, 1939 flying his Red 1 during the so-called *Luftschlacht über den Deutschen Bucht* (air battle over the German Bight). The machine is still finished in the dark green splinter scheme. The "seagull" Staffel badge forward of the cockpit would soon be replaced with a more warlike eagle.

a lot from your first victory. It is undoubtedly the most important of a fighter pilot's career. I was also lucky with the claim confirmation: I needed two witnesses, one on the ground and the other in the air. Finding a witness on the ground for a dogfight over the sea is rare. Fortunately, this was not the case for me: my victory was witnessed by the sailors of a *Zerstörer* [destroyer]. Their report being in perfect agreement with that transmitted to the O.K.L. [Oberkommando der Luftwaffe], my victory was approved.

This 6./JG 77 Emil displays the Staffel emblem forward of the cockpit: a penguin urinating on the initials W.C. "*Ein Pinguin gibt dem Lügenbaron W.C. die angemessene Antwort.*" The "lying baronet" was of course Winston Churchill.

Lt. Harald Jung of 1./JG 20 was the first *Jagdflieger* to shoot down a Spitfire, on March 22, 1940.

After this bloodletting, Bomber Command abandoned long-range daylight raids, taking refuge in night operations, until 1944.

On December 22, 1939, the Luftwaffe encountered British fighters for the first time: Hurricanes of 73 Squadron. A detachment of III./JG 53 dove on them and two were shot down by Kommander Mölders and the Kapitän of 8./JG 53, Hptm. Hans von Hahn, a rare engagement since London sent its fighters only sparingly to the Continental mainland.

With snow grounding most aircraft, relative calm prevailed in early 1940. Eleven German pilots claimed only 12 victories during January/February. One of these went to Spanish veteran Reinhard Seiler (1./JG 54), his first after nine in Spain, a Potez reconnaissance machine shot down in early January.

As Kommandeur II./JG 77, Oberstleutnant Carl Schumacher had been appointed Jagdfliegerführer Deutsche Bucht (Jafü Deutsche Bucht—Fighter Commander German Bight) in October 1939 to control all the disparate fighter units stationed on the northern coast. In November he was then given orders to set up a brand-new Geschwader. Initially (and unusually) comprising just a Stab or HQ Flight, called Stab./JG Nord, it was soon officially authorized as JG 1 on November 30, 1939, with Schumacher as its Kommodore. Here he is seen in the cockpit of his Bf 109 E-3 displaying the "Eagle over the German Bight" emblem.

Lt. Heinz Demes (4./JG 77) returns from a successful mission. He achieved three victories—including a Blenheim recce machine shot down over the North Sea on March 27—before being killed in Norway on April 30, 1940. Note the 4. Staffel emblem—the "*Sensenmann*," a skeleton riding a scythe.

Aerial activity resumed in March with around 20 victories. On the 3rd, by claiming a Morane, Hptm. Mölders achieved five victories. Oblt. Bretnütz (6./JG 53) claimed his fifth on March 30. Of note during this period was the first loss of a Spitfire when, on March 22, Lt. Harald Jung (1./JG 20) achieved his first *Luftsieg* near Klève, downing a reconnaissance aircraft of this type.

There were only 18 German claims in the West in April 1940 as the eyes of the world were on Scandinavia. From May 1 to 9, only four victories were claimed over the north of the Reich—only two were confirmed.

Weserübung: The Norwegian Campaign

With the "Phoney War" dragging on, the Western Allies tried to take the initiative. As the Reich depended on the supply of Swedish iron ore, an Allied landing was scheduled in Norway for April 8, 1940. But the day before, the Wehrmacht, which had anticipated this action, launched *Weserübung*—the invasion of Denmark and Norway. Given the large distances to be covered, the Bf 110, with better range, supplanted the Bf 109. II./JG 77 was the only single-engine fighter Gruppe in the area to counter the intrusions of RAF Coastal Command aircraft from coastal aerodromes. Indeed, several Wellingtons and Hudsons were shot down in the Stavanger area. During April, Lt. Edgar Struckmann and Fw. Robert Menge, of 5./JG 77, both returned their first four *Abschüsse*.

In conclusion, if the "Phoney War" may have seemed like this to the forces on the ground, this was not the case for many airmen. While the Polish and Norwegian air forces were easily dominated, from mid-September 1939 to May 9, 1940, dogfights between the Luftwaffe and the Armée de l'air were commonplace, with RAF fighters only deployed sparingly. During this period, those veterans of Spain cemented their reputations, bringing their experience to younger pilots, who, as future aces, won their first victories during these weeks of comparative respite.

The Campaign in the West, 1940

On May 10, 1940, the Wehrmacht launched *Westfeldzug*, the great campaign in the West, which some still misleadingly refer to as the "Battle of France." By invading the neutral nations of Netherlands, Belgium, and the Grand Duchy of Luxembourg, the Germans were able to lure the Franco-British armies to the north and then, in a feint, cut them off from their rear. This plan was overwhelmingly a success, as France collapsed like a house of cards.

To achieve this exceptionally bold movement, the Reich deployed most of its military resources. Twenty-nine single-engine fighter Gruppen took part (1,266 Bf 109s, including 897 in flight condition). The first few days saw the destruction of the small Dutch and Belgian air arms, on the ground or in the air. German fighters, sometimes surprised by the slowness and maneuverability of some biplanes, lost crew. But, these episodes were isolated and many future aces were able to open their scores with "easy prey," such as Hans-Ekkehard Bob, Gerhard Homuth, and Erbo Graf von Kageneck. Pilots of I./JG 1 were able to play catch-up. On May 11, Wilhelm Balthasar—who had missed the Polish campaign—claimed no fewer than four victories and, on May 12, Walter Adolph claimed four more. On the same day, May 12, Hptm. Adolf Galland arrived at I./JG 27.

Recently established III./JG 53 assemble for a group photo with their Kommandeur, Hptm. Mölders (back row, seated, hands in pockets).

Austrian Lt. Walter "Jap" Schneider of 5./JG 26, won his first two victories in the West in May 1940. He was appointed Staffelkapitän 6./JG 26 at the height of the Battle of Britain on September 20, 1940 and reached 20 victories (with nine "probables" marked "*nicht anerkannte Abschüsse*" in his logbook), but was killed in a crash in northern France on December 22, 1941. He is seen here, around May 12, 1940, on a field strip in Belgium, clowning around after finding a bugle and a boater. Note the "diving raven" emblem just under the cockpit of Black 6.

When advancing through France, the Tagjagd were mostly flying from field strips. Below, a line-up of II./JG 3 Emils.

On May 14 Spain veteran Oblt. Hans-Karl Mayer of 1./JG 53 claimed five RAF light bombers downed in just 12 minutes.

Very quickly, the Luftwaffe came up against the French Air Force and the RAF, but the German pilots regularly increased their scores at the expense of the fleets of obsolete bombers hurriedly thrown into the battle. On May 14, dubbed the "day of the fighters," no fewer than 120 victories were claimed by heavy (Bf 110) and single-engine (Bf 109) fighters; I./JG 53 led by Hptm. von Janson reported no fewer than 39 enemy aircraft shot down. Among the victims were 25 Fairey Battles and 11 Bristol Blenheims. Even if these figures were slightly high, they were still impressive. On a fighter sweep from his German base at Kirchberg late that afternoon Oblt. Hans-Karl Mayer of 1./JG 53 claimed five downed in just 12 minutes as the defenders threw everything into the Sedan "funnel."

Covering the advance of Rommel's 7th Panzer Division in its push towards Cambrai on May 17/18 was I./JG 77. After strafing aircraft based at Cambrai-Niergnies early in the morning, Oblt. Ehrig and Lt. Bauer shot down an M.S.406 and a Hurricane respectively during free-hunt sorties. On May 18, I./JG 77 claimed five Hurricanes and one Potez 63 in the course of different sorties. Two victories went to Ofw. Leyerer, a Hurricane and a Potez, possibly Po 637 No. 10 of GAR II/52 carrying out a reconnaissance in the evening for the French Ninth Army. Attacked by three Bf 109s, the crew bailed out before their aircraft exploded. The other victors were all "names," or about to become so: Fw. Adolf Borchers (first victory for this future Knight's Cross bearer), Oblt. Karl-Gottfried Nordmann (second victory for this future Oak Leaves bearer), Lt. Hubert Mütherich (second victory for this future Knight's Cross bearer), and Oblt. Priebe (Staffelkapitän 2./JG 77).

Individual scores mounted quickly: on May 20, Oblt. Wolfgang Lippert (3./JG 53) won his sixth victory and Ofw. Werner Machold (1./JG 2) his fifth. Mölders had 13 and Galland seven, and the next day Mölders reached 15 while H. Bretnütz shot down his seventh. On May 23, Balthasar reached ten victories.

Lt. Günther Rall of 8./JG 52, who had joined the army in 1936 at the age of 18 and was transferred to the Luftwaffe in 1938, returned his first victory on May 18 on an escort sortie for a 4./KG 27 Heinkel 111 reconnaissance aircraft over Nancy. He recalled:

> The French, a dozen of them, were targeting the Heinkel lower than us. There were ten of us and we fell on them. It was a hell of a mess. I was bathed in sweat! There were planes all over the place. I framed one of the Curtisses in my sight and let him have my first salvo at good range, but I had to pull up immediately. Just as I was about to turn into another Curtiss, my 109 was hit in the belly. I broke off. I didn't know where I was and all of a sudden I was afraid I wouldn't find my way back and

> would run out of gas. I oriented myself with the sun, and I headed on the opposite course to the one we had before the melee ... We had lost one of our own, Obfw. Adolf Walter. Walter wasn't an ace, but he was a very reliable comrade you could count on. He made an emergency landing. Climbing out of his machine, there were explosions going off all around him. He started running towards the Heer infantrymen who shouted at him: "Get down on your stomach!" Walter threw himself flat on the ground ... He must have had three times as many guardian angels as all of us because he'd landed in a minefield.

But these many successes, due to the good quality of the machines and the excellent training of the pilots, should not indicate that the campaign in the West was a "walkover" for the Luftwaffe. Every Gruppe regularly lost men and aircraft. These were by no means the least experienced.

On 15 May two II./JG 52 Messerschmitts were downed by Hurricanes between Namur and Dinant. The Kommandeur I./JG 52, Hptm. Siegfried von Eschwege, put down on his belly at Liège, while Lt. Kurt Kirchner (T.O.) bailed out and was captured at Charleville-Mézières, rejoining his unit on June 30, 1940.

On May 19, the Kommandeur of II./JG 26, Hptm. Herwig Knüppel (eight victories in Spain), was killed near Valenciennes. On the same day, one of his Staffelkapitäne was also lost.

On May 21, the Gruppenkommandeur III./JG 2 Maj. Erich Mix was shot down by Sous-Lieutenant Hubert de Salaberry in his GC I/3 Dewoitine D.520. Mix had just downed the D.520 flown by Sous-Lieutenant Jean Parisse (although he identified it as an M.S.406). De Salaberry left the following account:

> I dropped down in behind the "Fritz." He had seen me and understood straight away that the hunter was now the prey. He did what all German fighters do when they are caught napping—he rolled onto his back and dropped like a stone, counting on being able to build up enough speed to put some distance between us. I was not about to let him go. I rolled with him and headed down vertically, my engine screaming with the throttle against the stop. I had full confidence in my aircraft, the Dewoitine was very stable and the engine & prop behaved themselves impeccably ... Reeling the 109 slowly in during our headlong dive I unleashed several brief bursts from directly astern. The German pilot did not react and continued on down. Suddenly I noticed the sky becoming darker, realized that the ground was rushing up toward us. Crushed by the deceleration as I eased out the dive, I lost sight of the German. I orbited the area but could see nothing. Below me the countryside was peaceful and unremarkable.

At the end of May, the BEF, feeling the wind turning, withdrew to the beaches of La Panne/Dunkirk to embark for England. The Luftwaffe was ordered to engage in combat on the coast. For the first time Göring's men were confronted with Spitfire units from the other side of the Channel attempting to form a protective umbrella over the area and the fighting was fierce.

Farther east, at Lor/La Selve airfield III./JG 53 celebrated the award of the Knight's Cross to Kommandeur Mölders, the first Tagjäger to have achieved 20 victories (in addition to his 14 in Spain) and the first fighter pilot to receive the Knight's Cross.

Elsewhere on May 26, 1940, I./ZG 2—now in Neufchateau flying twin-engine Bf 110 C Zerstörer aircraft—suffered a nuisance raid by a pair of RAF Blenheims. Maj. Gentzen and his gunner, Oblt. Domeier, raced for one of the serviceable Bf 110s on the airfield to give chase to the fleeing RAF bombers. In their haste to make a quick takeoff, neither man had strapped in. As their machine strained to get airborne, it clipped the tops of the trees bordering the end of the airfield. The aircraft cartwheeled into the ground, fatally injuring both airmen. Although they were pulled from the wreckage, both died in the aftermath of the crash. At the time of his death, Gentzen was only just behind Mölders in the scoring stakes, with some 18 successes in air combat. He thus never won the Knight's Cross.

With the bloody British evacuation at La Panne/Dunkirk completed at the beginning of June, the Wehrmacht was able to embark on the real "Battle of France," the descent southwards. Throughout the first ten days of June, the list of claims continued to lengthen. On the 6th, there were 86 German victories, most of them in the opposing resistance sectors: Ham, Roye, and Amiens. Some British aircraft continuing the fight on the Continent (mainly bombers) were also claimed.

The day before, III./JG 53 had achieved significant successes (claiming 11 victories) but also experienced a serious setback. In the afternoon, the unit clashed with GC II/7 D.520s as Second Lieutenant René Pomier-Layrargues lined up on the enemy formation leader and unleashed a burst. His opponent was the recent Knight's Cross winner. Mölders belly-landed near Compiègne and was immediately captured. Apparently he expressed the wish to meet his victor but the latter had been shot down a few minutes after his success (probably by Gerhard Homuth, future *Experte* of JG 27).

On June 7, this time against the RAF, JG 26 lost two pilots. One of them was killed while the other, Lt. Klaus Mietusch, future ace of the "Schlageter," was captured in Offranville.

From June 11 to 24, the numbers of claims decreased. The last French aircraft shot down in combat was reportedly a Po 63 which "crashed" in Montélimar, victim of an unknown Bf 109 pilot. On June 14, 1940, Hptm. Wilhelm Balthasar was awarded the Knight's Cross.

The campaign in the West was an unexpected success for the Wehrmacht. At the end of this massive operation, many German aces had cut their teeth: Adolf

On May 27, 1940, after his 20th victory, a French Curtiss H-75 southwest of Amiens, Mölders was decorated with the Knight's Cross.

On May 26, 1940, Obfw. Werner Machold (1./JG 2) returned his eighth victory, a Spitfire near Calais. Here he is at the controls of his White 15.

Lt. Hans Krug (5./JG 26) had an unusual CV. Born in 1899 in Nuremberg (and therefore rather old for a fighter pilot), he had joined the Spanish nationalist air force of his own accord in October 1936 and fought throughout the civil war. He was credited with one kill before returning nine further victories in the Luftwaffe. Here he is wearing the Iron Cross awarded for his first three victories in May 1940. He was captured in England on September 7, 1940. Sent to a POW camp in Canada, he escaped on April 16, 1942 and reached San Antonio, Texas, around May 1, 1942 where he was arrested and sent back to Canada. A restaurant owner in Detroit, Michigan, helped Krug during his escape and for this he was sentenced to life in prison.

On June 1, 1940, on a transfer flight, Uffz. Artur Beese (9./JG 26) got lost, landed near Chauny and was captured by French troops. He was released at the end of the campaign in the West but was killed on February 6, 1944 in France, credited with 22 victories.

JG 26 Bf 109s en route to Villacoublay fly over Paris, a striking symbol of the victory of German arms.

At Signy-le-Petit, Hptm. Alexander von Winterfeldt (leading 3./JG 2) returned with a victory on May 20. He was an "old man" of the Great War like Mix or von Bülow.

Galland had 14 kills, Rolf Pingel eight *Luftsiege* and so on. This is not counting all the other credits from five to eight *Abschüsse*. Even a veteran of the Great War, Alexander von Winterfeldt, had returned five victories to add to the four that he had achieved with Jasta 20 in 1918.

Helmut Wick at the controls of his 3./JG 2 Bf 109. He returned his 11th kill on June 8 and downed a Blenheim the next day northeast of Soissons. He wrote, "I am now the leading pilot in the Geschwader, ahead even of the excellent Ofw. Machold."

All this was not achieved without cost. By the end of June 1940, the Luftwaffe had sustained heavy losses. Britain was still refusing any offer of peace. The assumption of a long campaign in France meant that *Fall Gelb* (Case Yellow), the invasion plans for the West, included no provision for the invasion of England. Worse still, infrastructure (ports, airfields) along the Channel coast essential for the continued prosecution of the war had been severely damaged. There had been little preparation—shipping, crews, landing barges—for an invasion across the Channel. There was no real prospect of a landing taking place much before March 1941. The government in London would have to be forced into a compromise peace by means of air power alone.

Between 650 and 1,000 Luftwaffe aircraft were lost during the campaign in the West. Losses on the opening day of the invasion—May 10—exceeded the biggest daily loss during the fighting over England later that summer. Included in the total losses were around 165 Bf 109s shot down and a further 50 or so lost in accidents. Messerschmitt Regensburg was only producing around 25 new Bf 109s a month during this period. Some French historians maintain that this French contribution to the "Battle of Britain" was decisive. It almost certainly accounts for the Luftwaffe's six-week pause before setting out to subdue England. Seen here are two downed Emils of JG 27.

| Over England, 1940

The "Battle of Britain" would provide a stiff test for the Luftwaffe. As some have pointed out, the problems were as much technical as they were human. The Luftwaffe's task in the summer of 1940 was very different from the one planned in the 1930s. It had to adapt quickly, from its role of supporting a land army to an air force engaged against another very well-armed air force. This change caused many logistical problems.

A network of aerodrome and airfield infrastructure had to be set up throughout northern France. Some former French bases could certainly be put back into service, but they had to be supplied with fuel, spare parts, ordnance, and rations beforehand. Maintenance was difficult to organize and many aircraft were sent back to the Reich for overhaul. To overcome these problems, the German fighter force had to be divided into various commands. But these units were at an additional disadvantage because this fighter force, once assembled, could no longer be directed once airborne. There was another important factor at play: by the end of May, the British secret services were able to decrypt, thanks to Ultra, all Luftwaffe Enigma communications, so that in many instances planned raids by the Luftwaffe could be countered. The fighting over England during 1940 can be divided into four phases:

Josef Priller claimed his first kill during the Battle of Britain with 6./JG 51 on July 14, 1940 and his twentieth on October 17, resulting in the award of the Knight's Cross two days later.

Hptm. Adolf Galland flew this E-4 on two days in August—August 12 and 14—claiming his 17th (a Hurricane, north of Margate) and 18th victories. Note the 9./JG 26 "Hellhound" Staffel emblem. He had been appointed Kommandeur III./JG 26 on June 11, 1940 and would be promoted Kommodore JG 26 with the rank of Major on August 20.

Phase 1: Waiting

While most of the JGs returned to the Reich, the RAF attacked French airfields. Thus, on June 25, Oblt. Josef Priller claimed a Spitfire near Desvres. On the 27th, five Blenheims were shot down by the Kommandeur I./JG 54, Hptm. Hubertus von Bonin, and two other pilots. A sixth, chased by Hptm. Horst Tietzen, Kapitän of 5./JG 51, was shot down south of Dover.

The Luftwaffe then attacked. The bombers initially operated at night, the fighters "testing the water" during the day. On July 4, nine Hurricanes were surprised by Bf 109s over Dungeness, with two being shot down (one claim by Lt. Geisshardt). On the evening of the 5th, three Spitfires patrolling northern France were intercepted by 4./JG 51, claiming two victories (Lt. Erich Hohagen and Ofw. Johann Illner). Overall, Fighter Command remained prudent.

July 10, 1940 is the day designated by the British as the beginning of the Battle of Britain. On the 16th, Adolf Hitler promulgated Directive No. 16: Operation *Seelöwe*. The Luftwaffe was tasked with persuading London to sue for peace. On July 19, Hitler launched a "last appeal to reason" to the British people, rejected three days later. The fighting would continue.

July 24 saw a fierce clash over the Channel. The Bf 109 pilots would come to fully "appreciate" the Achilles heel of their machines: their limited endurance. While two victories were attributed to III./JG 26—including the 14th for Maj. Adolf Galland, who was appointed Kommandeur—Hptm. Erich Noack, leading II./JG 26, brought back his damaged 109 but was killed crash-landing at Marquise.

Seen here as Staffelkapitän of 3./JG 26 (until February 29, 1940), the Kommandeur of III./JG 52 Hptm. von Houwald, a five-victory ace in Spain, was shot down and killed on his first sortie over England.

Having only arrived at Coquelles on the Channel coast west of Calais on July 22, III./JG 52 flew a diversionary sortie over Dover but lost their Kommandeur, Hptm. Wolf-Heinrich von Houwald, and two Staffelkapitäne.

On July 28, the RAF lost three Spitfires and a single Hurricane; the Tagjagd three JG 51 machines. Two further Bf 109s managed to limp back to France, one of them being that of Maj. Werner Mölders, the recently appointed Kommodore. However, he recovered quickly while, on the 29th, Galland was finally awarded the Knight's Cross for his 17th victory.

On the last day of July, an important meeting was held at Berchtesgaden where the invasion of the USSR was discussed. The pressure was on to shut down the Western Front.

Uffz. Kurt Hübel of 7./JG 51 borne aloft from his Bf 109 after returning his first victory on July 11. He claimed a Spitfire shot down over Dungeness on September 14. He was shot down and killed over London on September 30.

Phase 2: The Offensive

On August 1, no convoys were attacked, the Luftwaffe now preserving its bombers. On August 1 the order was given to intensify operations to destroy the enemy fighter arm.

On August 8, the Kommandeur II./JG 27, Hptm. Werner Andres, was shot down over the Channel. While he managed to bail out, he was adrift for hours. After his eventual rescue, he was taken off operations for a lengthy spell. On August 1, 1941 he was named Kommandeur III./JG 3 but was injured in a takeoff accident on August 28, 1941. On May 13, 1942 he was appointed Kommandeur ErgGr. Ost. (Supplementary Fighter Group East).

On August 12, the Gruppenkommandeur of III./JG 53, Hptm. "Harro" Harder, failed to return from combat; his body washed ashore near Dieppe on September 13. Harder had accumulated 11 victories in Spain and had replaced Mölders at the head of JG 53. He shot down three Spitfires on August 11 for his victories 18–20 and his comrades assigned two more victories to him on August 12, the day he was killed. His total was estimated at twenty-two.

On August 13, a small force of 12 82 Sqn Blenheims set out from RAF Watton to raid the Danish airfield base of Aalborg: of the 11 machines that reached Aalborg all 11 were shot down, 5./JG 77 filing 15 claims. Four were credited to Ofw. Robert Menge for his kills 10–13. Unurprisingly, the raid received little UK press coverage.

On the German side August 13 was significant—*Adlertag* or Eagle Day. But in deciding to launch this type of "big blow" against England, the Luftwaffe played into the hands of the RAF: with such operations requiring lengthy preparations, thanks to Ultra, the RAF knew the targets beforehand and had the time to organize its defenses. Large bomber formations had to be covered by an escort, which limited fighter vs. fighter combat when it might otherwise have proved favorable to the Bf 109s. Oblt. Johannes Steinhoff's 4./JG 52 was one Staffel ordered to fly close-escort missions over England to "better" protect the German bombers. Steinhoff's comments in his memoirs are telling: 'Stay at any price with the bombers, do not take up the battle with the Spitfires,' read our directives. 'Do not be lured into combat even if you are in an ideal firing position.' This was something that made us young fighter pilots start to despair … our protégés dragged themselves along at walking pace."

Because of this tactic Bf 109 pilots were at a disadvantage against the RAF fighters, who dove on them from above with the advantage of speed and height. It meant foregoing one of the Messerschmitt 109's major advantages—its speed. The Bf 109 E was probably just superior to the Spitfire Mk I and Hurricane in terms of speed of climb and dive and had heavier firepower. Used correctly, they might have beaten Fighter Command in spite of the Luftwaffe's many failings, and yet this advantage was uselessly thrown away. The fighter pilots felt this keenly and unsurprisingly morale began to drop. As noted by Günther Rall: "By ordering us to fly as close escorts, our Gruppe was effectively offered up on a plate to the most efficient and determined aerial opponents the Luftwaffe had yet come up against."

By August 16, 1940, after only five days of fighting over the English Channel, Steinhoff's 4./JG 52 had claimed seven enemy fighters for the loss of six Bf 109s and three pilots. The unit was considered exhausted and there was no other option than to take it out of the battle. The unit returned to operations on September 20 for a second spell, claiming another

In Profile:
Bf 109s 1937–1940

Bf 109 A coded 6-10 of 2.J/88 commanded by Oblt. Werner Lützow. Beneath the cockpit is the laurel wreath marking Lützow's first victory, the first ever by a Bf 109 pilot, returned on April 6, 1937. Aft of 2./JG 88's "top hat" is painted a face quaffing from a mug of foaming beer with the admonishment "*Pass uff*" or "Watch it!" Note the wooden fixed-pitch two-bladed propeller.

Bf 109 Dora in JGr. 102 (subordinated to I./ZG 2) flown by Hptm. Johannes Gentzen, Gruppenkommandeur and the leading Luftwaffe fighter pilot over Poland. Gentzen claimed seven victories between September 2 and September 14, 1939. Note the white victory markings on the tailfin of his "White Chevron Triangle," which features both Gruppe and Staffel emblems.

Messerschmitt Bf 109 E-4 of III./JG 3 "Fortuna," France 1940, flown by Hptm. Walter Kienitz. A Condor Legion veteran, Kienitz was Gruppenkommandeur III./JG 3 during the campaign in the West but was removed from command during the Battle of Britain and replaced by Wilhelm Balthasar, the leading ace of the French campaign. Kienitz's Emil is finished in the standard 71/02/65 scheme.

16 RAF fighters, at a cost of 16 more 109s, with three pilots killed and another nine taken prisoner. It is therefore not surprising that on the evening of *Adlertag*, German losses were for the first time much higher than those of the enemy (about 40 aircraft against 20).

On August 15, the Luftwaffe tried to erase this failure. Once again, thanks to Ultra, the advantage was with the British camp (66 German losses and 31 British).

Fighter pilots on escort duties were chafing at the bit. When they could operate freely, they showed their qualities, as on August 16 during a "duel" over Deal. If the Spitfires surprised their adversaries and shot down the Kommandeur II./JG 26, Hptm. Karl Ebbighausen, the rest of the unit decimated 266 Sqn.

While the Tagjagd was recording victories, attrition was taking its toll. On August 18, Staffelkapitän 9./JG 26 Oblt. Gerd Schöpfel downed four 501 Sqn Hurricanes in as many minutes, taking his score to 12 victories. He would be appointed Kommandeur III./JG 26 in a matter of days. That afternoon Hptm. Horst Tietzen, another Condor Legion ace and Kapitän of 5./JG 51, was shot down off the Kent coast along with his *Rottenflieger*, his wingman, Lt. Hans Lessing. With his score at five on July 10, Tietzen had subsequently returned 14 more victories. He was credited with his final and 20th on his death. The Knight's Cross was awarded to him posthumously two days later. The bodies of both airmen were washed ashore in France.

On the 20th, Hptm. Walter Oesau of 7./JG 51 received the Knight's Cross. He also reached the 20-victory mark, in addition to seven won in Spain. Promoted Kommandeur of III./JG 51, he became one of the great Tagjagd aces. Two days later, the Knight's Cross was also awarded to Oberstleutnant von Bülow (leading JG 2) and Generalmajor Osterkamp. Osterkamp had six victories to his credit in addition to his 32 successes achieved during the Great War. Born in 1892 and 48 years old, Osterkamp was one of the oldest Luftwaffe aces at the start of the war. Von Bülow (six victories in 1917/18) scored no victories in 1939/40. The Knight's Cross was in these instances reward for effective leadership of their units in the fierce fighting in the West. However, these old leaders would soon be replaced with younger and, it was hoped, more dynamic men; in the Luftwaffe fighter arm: "He who cannot kill, did not lead for long."

Nine victories on the rudder of a 109 during the Battle of Britain.

Staffelkapitän 5./JG 51 Hptm. Horst "Jakob" Tietzen in his Bf 109 E Red 1.

Hptm. Horst Tietzen (left) with his Kommodore, former Great War ace Theo Osterkamp. Both were awarded the Knight's Cross, Tietzen for 20 victories and Osterkamp for the good conduct of the unit.

Tietzen's wingman, Lt. Hans Lessing, climbing out of his Emil at Mardyck.

The friendly ties between Helmut Wick and the Reichsmarschall are in evidence in this photograph taken during a visit by Göring to JG 2 at Cherbourg-Querqueville during the late summer of 1940. Standing between the Richthofen aces of 1918 and 1940 is Luftwaffe Chief of Staff General Hans Jeschonnek.

On August 22 a new Kommodore was appointed to JG 26 in the person of Adolf Galland. Like Mölders, Wick, and Joppien, he had become one of the darlings of the Reich propaganda services.

On August 26, a new tactic was adopted: attacking British airfields by saturating the defenses. Losses were fairly evenly matched because, even if the RAF knew the enemy objectives of the day, it lacked the pilots to effectively defend them all. On August 27, Göring's "protégé," Wick, was awarded the Knight's Cross for 22 victories.

On August 28, Oblt. Franz von Werra, Gruppen-adjutant II./JG 3, claimed to have a carried out a daring solitary attack on a Hurricane squadron, shooting down three as they were setting up for a landing and then strafing and destroying five machines on the ground. Despite a lack of witnesses, von Werra's claims were apparently accepted as

A future ace of JG 26, Karl "Charly" Willius returned his first victory with 8./JG 51 on August 18, a Spitfire over Ramsgate.

On September 5, 1940, Oblt. Franz von Werra had to belly-land his Bf 109 E-4 (W.Nr. 1480) on English soil. Note the black-white segmented spinner.

his victories six through eight, at least at unit level, making August 28 the most successful day for II./JG 3 during the Battle of Britain. Barely a week later, on September 5, after an escort mission, he was bounced by Spitfires and forced to belly-land at Winchet Hill, south of London. He was determined to evade capture and captivity but all three of his attempts failed, including at least one that involved stealing an aircraft after brazenly walking onto an RAF base.

On August 30, having just arrived on the Channel coast, I./JG 77 lost two Staffelkapitäne. Flying out of Marquise, Oblt. Jürgen Ehrig of 1./JG 77 and Oblt. Ekkehard Priebe of 2. Staffel were shot down over Kent and taken captive on one of the first missions flown by the Gruppe during the battle. Fw. Adolf Borchers bailed out over the Channel but was saved

Von Werra's scoreboard: eight aerial victories and five aircraft destroyed on the ground (arrows pointing down).

by his wingman, Lt. Heinz Escherhaus, who drove off a British rescue launch and guided in a *Seenot*, a sea-rescue aircraft. Borchers continued a career that would be crowned with a Knight's Cross.

The air battles over southern England reached a climax on August 31, as the *Jagdflieger* claimed 82 victories. No fewer than four were filed by Hptm. Ernst Wiggers of 2./JG 51. His Staffel comrade Ofw. Fritz Ströhlein filed three. However, 13-victory ace Wiggers would be shot down and killed in the vicinity of Lewes, Sussex, on September 11.

On September 2, Oblt. von Bülow handed over command of JG 2 to Wolfgang Schellmann, the second "Spanish" ace behind Mölders. To "rejuvenate" his fighter leaders, Göring gradually withdrew all World War I veterans (like Osterkamp) from the front. Elsewhere, Lt. Heinz Bär (I./JG 51) was shot down over the Channel. Rescued from the sea, he resumed combat with his unit … and continued to fly combat sorties until May 1945.

On the 4th, I./JG 2 claimed six victories. In addition to the *Experten* (Machold, Bertram, or Rudorffer), the unit nurtured talented future aces, such as Uffz. Kurt Bühligen, who opened his score that day during his 18th combat flight, one of many of that unit's recipients of the Knight's Cross.

On the 3rd and 5th, this decoration was awarded respectively to Hptm. Hans-Karl Mayer (20 victories in addition to his eight in Spain), recently appointed Kommandeur of I./JG 53, and Ofw. Werner Machold (21 victories) of JG 2.

By September 5, the Luftwaffe was on the way to "statistically" winning the Battle of Britain. However, attrition was wearing it down as much as the RAF; continued losses risked

Bf 109s of 4./JG 3 under the trees at Wierre-au-Bois, southeast of Boulogne-sur-Mer on the Channel coast during late August 1940. Staffelkapitän Lt. Richard von Larisch was shot down and killed over London on August 31, 1940.

Oblt. Gustav Sprick, Staffelkapitän of 8./JG 26, about to get airborne for another sortie over England.

jeopardizing the planned assault on the Soviet Union. So until the British surrendered—an unlikely scenario—the Luftwaffe continued to lose men and machines to little purpose. As the summer wore on, these factors all contributed to mounting cases of what was becoming termed *Kanalkrankheit*—Channel Sickness—better known now as combat fatigue. As Ulrich Steinhilper noted: "Although most of us were still not outwardly showing major signs of nerves, by late August arguments were becoming more frequent, tempers frayed quicker … The strain of unrelenting front-line flying was beginning to show."

On September 7, the Luftwaffe turned its attentions toward London.

Phase 3: Over London

The Luftwaffe played its last card. But here again the RAF held the upper hand: warned by Ultra, the RAF was able to concentrate its defensive resources around the capital; and the Bf 109 escorts had only a limited endurance, being able to loiter for only 15 minutes over the city.

On September 7, the first day of raids on London, the Germans overwhelmed the defenses. Fighter Command lost 33 aircraft. On the German side, a dozen bombers were lost as well as 15 Bf 109s and ten Bf 110s. On the 8th, the Luftwaffe could not repeat its previous day's effort and the RAF accepted a breathing space. On the 9th, orders were given to bomb the capital day and night. Two major raids took place in the afternoon, but here the Luftwaffe could no longer saturate the defense. Nevertheless, 23 fighters were downed by Bf 109s. The Staffelkapitän 4./JG 53, Oblt. Günther Schulze-Blanck who had led the Staffel from August 1940, was killed in a dogfight over Hastings. He had returned six victories. His body washed up on a French beach some two weeks later.

There was by now perhaps, a growing realization that the fighter pilots had been assigned an impossible task. Lt. Jules Meimberg of 4./JG 2:

> It was not until today that I grasped just how big a city London is. Brussels, Paris, even Berlin are tiny in comparison. What sort of effect could we hope to achieve with a few hundred bombs on a metropolis like this, aside from inflicting a few scratches?

On September 11, the fighting was particularly costly with the Luftwaffe claiming 67 fighters, while RAF Fighter Command claimed 89 German aircraft. Actual losses however amounted

to 30 RAF fighters and 27 Luftwaffe machines—11 bombers, eight Bf 110s and about eight Bf 109s including the machine flown by a certain Fhr. (Fähnrich, or Flight Officer) Hans-Joachim Marseille (1./LG 2) who managed to return to Wissant to crash-land his machine, 75-percent destroyed.

Oblt. Ihlefeld, Kommandeur I./Lehrgeschwader 2, participated in this large-scale raid. In total, 280 bombers, supported by 750 fighters headed for the coast. During the clash Ihlefeld shot down a Spitfire at 17:05 and a Hurricane at 17:10. This took his total to 21 victories and two days later, on September 13, 1940, he was awarded the Knight's Cross. Appointed to lead 2.(J)/LG 2 during June 1940 as Staffelkapitän, he had returned his first on May 29, 1940 (a Morane 406) while flying with the Stab.

Further to other victories won at that time, there were a number of other Knight's Crosses awarded. On the 11th, two Bf 110 pilots were honored along with Hptm. Gerd Schöpfel. A former police officer, Schöpfel had succeeded Adolf Galland as head of III./JG 26 on 22 August 1940. He had just claimed three 92 Sqn Spitfires over the Thames Estuary on 9 September 1940, taking his score to 20 *Abschüsse*. On the 14th, Oblt. Joachim Müncheberg (Kapitän of the 7./JG 26, 20 victories) and Hptm. Rolf Pingel, Kommandeur I./JG 26 (15 victories plus six in Spain) received the Knight's Cross.

Above and below: Emils down on the coast. Note the red band around the cowl of the JG 53 Emil being recovered. The risk of running out of fuel meant that loiter time over England was limited. The short endurance of the Bf 109 over England was its Achilles heel.

On September 15, the weather cleared and the Luftwaffe prepared for their "final blow" against England. This was to be the test of strength for Göring's Luftwaffe and Dowding's refreshed and reinforced Fighter Command. During the day's prolonged and bitter fighting the Luftwaffe would lose 6 percent of their committed forces—57 aircraft—their highest percentage loss rate during the entire Battle of Britain. With the RAF's rather moderate losses of 26–28 fighters, this day would later celebrated by the British as "Battle of Britain Day." It was nevertheless a good day for Oblt. Helmut Bennemann of 2./JG 52 flying his Bf 109 Emil Black 5 who recorded three Hurricanes shot down, all of them over the Thames Estuary. These were his sixth through eighth *Abschüsse*, and he was ultimately credited with 93 victories in over 400 missions, with 77 of these on the Eastern Front.

Fighter Command's losses were half of those on the German side, i.e. the rates of the *Adlertag* of 13 August. To the OKW, it now appeared that in major offensives, the RAF was always able to pull out the stops and many more weeks would be required to destroy the RAF. After a review of tactics, it was decided to raid RAF aerodromes and factories directly.

On the 16th, Oblt. Hermann-Friedrich Joppien, Kapitän of 1./JG 51, was awarded the Knight's Cross (21 victories).

On the 18th, two veterans of Spain were honored: Maj. Günther Lützow, Kommodore of JG 3, received the Knight's Cross for his 15 victories and Maj. Wolfgang Schellmann, leading JG 2, for his 11 *Abschüsse*.

A reduction in escort duties allowed the Tagjagd to return in force. On September 20, during two major fighter sweeps over Dover and Dungeness, Fighter Command lost seven aircraft at a cost of two Bf 109s, one each from 8./JG 3 and 9./JG 27.

On September 21, having been credited with 40 victories, Werner Mölders was awarded the Oak Leaves (to the Knight's Cross), the second Wehrmacht soldier to be so honored.

On September 23, ten more RAF fighters were downed. That day, Fhr. Marseille (1./LG 2) escaped death once again. Forced to ditch his Bf 109 in the Channel, the future ace survived for several hours at sea before being rescued. On the same day, the Kommodore of JG 26, Adolf Galland, obtained his 39th and 40th victories and was awarded the Oak Leaves soon afterward. Ofw. Gerhard Grzymalla of 8./JG 26 was taken captive when his Bf 109 E-4, Black 9 (W.Nr. 5817) was shot

Herbert Ihlefeld was awarded the Knight's Cross on September 13. Here he poses with his scorecard painted on the tailfin of his Emil at Calais-Marck on the Channel coast. Ihlefed was Kommandeur I./Lehrgeschwader 2.

down over Biddenden, south of London, by a Spitfire. He had returned his first victory in combat on 14 May and his seventh and last on 18 September. Also taken captive was JG 2's Uffz. Fritz Dilthey. Dilthey had been posted to the Geschwader in early 1940—as an aircraft mechanic. He was, however, a trained (civilian) pilot. Kapitän Hahn had immediately sent him off to get his military *Flugscheine*, or pilot's license. Although taken captive in England, Dilthey was more fortunate than his elder brother Helmut. Born in 1894, Helmut Dilthey was a seven-victory ace who had led Jasta 40 during the Great War—he was killed in combat near Lille on July 9, 1918.

On the 24th, German raids targeted aircraft production plants. Fighter Command lost ten aircraft for a single Bf 109. Two more aces were awarded the Knight's Cross: Oblt. Hans Hahn, leading 4./JG 2, rewarded for his tenacity and 20th victory, and Hptm. Wolfgang Lippert, a veteran of Spain, recently appointed Kommandeur of II./JG 27 (13 *Abschüsse*).

On the 26th, the Luftwaffe targeted the Supermarine plants at Woolston. Fighter Command lost eight machines. A single Bf 109 was lost. On the other hand, on September 30, casualties were high on both sides, with Fighter Command losing 21 aircraft, the Luftwaffe 13 bombers and 28 Bf 109s, hampered by the obligation to provide close escort. In these battles on the 30th, Fighter Command's losses amounted to half those of the Luftwaffe's.

In late August I.(J)/LG 2 took delivery of their first Bf 109 E-4/B—a variant equipped with an ETC (electric carrier for cylindrical external stores) carrier rack for the carriage of 250-kg bombs, enabling *Jabo-Einsätze* (fighter-bomber sorties) to henceforth be flown against England. At that time the Staffel was based at Calais-Marck and Staffelkapitän Ihlefeld's Bf 109 E (W.Nr. 2030) Black 1 was likewise fitted with the new rack. The fact that each Gruppe had to designate such a Staffel would irritate Galland:

> I remember the helpless rage that seized me when I was ordered to have a third of my Gruppe transformed to fill the Jabo role. For months, we had been trying to lighten our aircraft to give them maximum maneuverability and now instead of supplementary fuel (or drop) tanks we were being sent bombs!

Of course, once each *Jabo* machine had dropped its ordnance, the aircraft assumed the classic fighter role. Contrary to Galland's vituperations, the *Jabo* totally surprised the RAF—a

Staffelkapitän 5./JG 3 Oblt. Herbert Kijewski in his Black 1 at Wierre-au-Bois. Note the inscription on the cowl just visible—"Erika," Kijewski's wife. This machine may be W.Nr. 1443, which crash-landed at Marquise with 75-percent damages on September 2.

"light" bomber attacking targets of opportunity could not be countered by exploiting the intelligence garnered from Ultra. For the Germans it was an innovation that came too late to make a difference to the outcome of the battle.

The *Jabo* offensive continued. On October 5, waves of Messerschmitt 109s (possibly as many as a hundred fighters), of which around 30 were toting ordnance, headed for Southampton and London. Fighter Command was no longer to be directed exclusively against German bombers: the Spitfires and Hurricanes were free to engage the Messerschmitts.

JG 2 was assigned to fly two escort missions for the Bf 110s of ZG 26 during the course of the afternoon and saw some of the hardest fighting, claiming at least 14 *Luftsiege*. In reality Fighter Command was to lose seven machines, while a further eight sustained damage. During the course of the fighting Kommandeur Wick claimed five *Abschüsse* for victories 37 through to 41, thus passing the 40 mark and resulting in the award—as the fourth soldier of the Wehrmacht—of the Oak Leaves to his Knight's Cross.

I./JG 2 flew a number of sweeps over the Portland–Southampton sector and subsequently filed a number of claims.

On the 11th, seven major raids were carried out, the *Jabos* targeting Biggin Hill, Ashford, and other airfields. Fighter Command lost 11 machines during the course of the day, while the only RAF victory of the day was the downing of a 5./JG 27 Bf 109.

On the 15th, good weather made it possible to attack London. In the morning, *Jabo* raids destroyed the tracks at Waterloo Station. The RAF lost some 20 machines for about ten Bf 109s.

On the 17th, the Luftwaffe again committed its fighters and *Jabos*, which appeared from out of the cloud cover. Six Fighter Command aircraft were shot down. But on that day, the Kommandeur of I./JG 53, Hptm. Karl Mayer, a recent Knight's Cross holder and former "Spaniard," was lost in unknown circumstances, apparently shot down, after taking off for an air-test. He was most probably caught up in clash with RAF fighters, but according to at least one German-language source, had taken off with unloaded magazines. His body was washed up on the beach near Dymchurch, west of Folkestone. He was subsequently buried in the cemetery at Hawkinge where he still lies, a rare Luftwaffe Knight's Cross bearer still on British soil. On October 19, Oblt. Josef "Pips" Priller, Kapitän of 6./JG 51, received the Knight's Cross for his 20 victories. A month later, he moved to JG 26 where he would make a name for himself.

A JG 53 *Jabo* at Le Touquet on the Channel coast south of Boulogne.

Another front page for a successful *Jagdflieger*—Wilhelm Balthasar on the cover of a late October 1940 edition of *Berlin Illustrirte Zeitung*.

On the 21st, Hptm. Dietrich Hrabak, the recently appointed Kommandeur of II./JG 54, was awarded the Knight's Cross after 16 *Luftsiege*.

On the morning of the 22nd, the Luftwaffe attacked maritime convoys, downing four fighters but losing three Bf 109s of JG 26, 27, and 51. On that day, Kommodore Werner Mölders, leading JG 51, claimed his first victory at the controls of a Bf 109 F, the latest variant still under test. It was not until the following year that the "Friedrich" gradually replaced the "Emil." And, on the same day, two new Knight's Crosses were awarded, to Hptm. Heinz Bretnütz, former member of the Condor Legion and Kapitän of 5./JG 53 (20 victories plus 12 balloons destroyed), and Oblt. Hans Philipp (20 victories).

Bf 109 E-4 (W.Nr. 1559) flown by the Kommandeur III./JG 3 Wilhelm Balthasar. This is the same aircraft Balthasar flew prior to being posted to JG 3, hence the Gruppe emblem of I./JG 1 (later III./JG 27) under the cockpit. It is just possible to make out the "White 1" on the engine cowling (placed on the ground). A Staffelkapitän's pennant is still present on the antenna mast.

October 1940 at Le Havre. Two JG 2 Knight's Cross bearers: Otto Bertram (left) and Werner Machold (right, partially hidden). Bertram would soon receive a *Flugverbot*, a flying ban.

On the 25th, the return of good weather allowed several raids to be launched, resulting in heavy Tagjagd losses with no fewer than 11 Bf 109s of JGs 26, 51, 53, 53, 54, and 77 failing to return. For its part, the RAF lost 11 machines.

Activity on both sides is evidenced by the number of RAF sorties. On October 27, no fewer than 1,007 took place, more than the 974 of 15 August 1940, which is explained by the new tactics of the *Jabos*/small formations of fighters.

On the 28th, Major Otto Bertram, a veteran of the Condor Legion (nine victories in Spain) and Kommandeur of III./JG 2, was awarded the Knight's Cross (for his 13 victories), but was soon withdrawn from the front following a *Führeranlass* (Führer decree), his two brothers having been killed during the Battle of Britain. Otto, the only survivor, was transferred to a training school and thus saw out the end of the war.

On the 29th, *Jabos* flew a raid against London, targeting Charing Cross bridge. They were caught by Hurricanes obstructing their movements and then Spitfires, at higher altitude, dove on them. Lt. Gerhard Barkhorn (6./JG 52) was forced to bail out into the English Channel. He was rescued after several hours and went on to a successful career.

Bad weather resulted in little activity on October 30. Fighter Command still lost eight machines to the Bf 109s. Adolf Galland claimed his 50th victory while four fighters from JG 3 and JG 26 were lost.

The rain-soaked October 31, the official date of the end of the Battle of Britain, saw no activity.

Phase 4: The Lull

Winter brought the recall of many units to the Reich. German bombers operated mainly at night in the Blitz. Enemy fighters had little chance of locating each other through the banks of clouds.

On November 5, Lt. Heinz Ebeling (leading 9./JG 26) was hit by his wingman in a *Jabo* mission and had to jump clear over Dungeness. Captured, he learned that on the very day of his misfortune he had been awarded the Knight's Cross for his 18 victories. It would be presented to him in his Canadian POW camp. On November 5, Oblt. Arnold Lignitz, leading III./JG 54, also received the Knight's Cross for his 19 victories. On the 9th, in turn, the young Lt. Siegfried Schnell (4./JG 2) won the Knight's Cross for 20 *Luftsiege*.

However, fighting was sustained when the weather allowed raids over England. On November 11, II./JG 53 faced off against RAF fighters, claiming five Spitfires and a Hurricane. Among the successful aces were the usual names: Brändle, Bretnütz, and Litjens.

Also on November 11, Oblt. Hans-Ekkehard Bob claimed his last victory during the Battle of Britain, a Spitfire that he shot down over Margate at 13:17. Later that month, Bob was appointed Staffelkapitän of 9./JG 54, a position which he held until August 1943.

On the 13th, Hptm. Walter Adolph, a sailor leading 8./JG 27, was awarded the Knight's Cross (16 victories). Hptm. Karl-Heinz Krahl, from the army and Kommandeur of I./JG 2 (15 victories) also received the award. Both were Condor Legion veterans: Adolph in fighters had been credited with one victory; Krahl in bombers had retrained on fighters on his return to Germany.

On November 23, Fw. Wurmheller (5./JG 53) had his aircraft so damaged in combat that he had to make an emergency landing for the second time in his career. After drifting for four hours in the Channel, he was rescued but was hospitalized for a lengthy spell.

On November 28, the leading fighter ace of the Luftwaffe took off from the Cotentin Peninsula for a free hunt over southern England. After shooting down a Spitfire early that afternoon, Helmut Wick's score stood at 55, one more than Werner Mölders. On returning to Cherbourg, Wick ordered his Emil refueled and re-armed and took off again for the south coast of England. Thirty-eight JG 2 aircraft were airborne from Cherbourg-West and Théville for that second operation of the day: a free hunt in the Southampton–Isle of Wight–Portsmouth area. Spitfires of 609 Sqn were waiting for them at altitude over the coast. Lt. Jules Meimberg led 4. Staffel that day:

> Just abeam of the Isle of Wight we reached an altitude of around 7,000 meters. In the freezing glass-clear atmosphere there appeared a fan of contrails heading towards us. The usual game was about to begin—the RAF knew at what height, from which direction and in what strength we were coming and were already waiting for us in extremely favorable conditions ... Wick leading off his Stabsschwarm at full

On November 28, Adolf Galland was credited with several victories. His 57th was a 249 Sqn Spitfire. This machine may well be W.Nr. 5819 which Galland flew on many occasions during late 1940 until around March 1941. Note the TZR telescopic sight visible in the Emil cockpit.

Lt. Jules Meimberg poses alongside his scoreboard during the early summer of 1940.

> throttle had considerably loosened our formation. My 4. Staffel was trailing off to one side. I kept one eye on the contrails as they gradually took the form of many glittering points of light, growing ever larger: Spitfires—diving in to the attack. The spinning carousel could start—dogfight! In no time at all we were caught up in a wild melee which immediately split the Staffel asunder. Out of the corner of my eye I caught sight of a Spitfire that I slipped in behind. He was pulling a tight turn but I managed to stick to his tail. Pulling back hard on the joystick, the leading edge slats popped out and the Englishman disappeared under my nose. A quick squeeze on the firing button, then release the stick so as not to stall. When the Spitfire reappeared in front of me, there was nothing to suggest that I had hit it. However, it tipped over on one wing before it pitched down. Convinced that it was a ruse to shake me off, I went after him, expecting to see him quickly regain altitude. However, the aircraft was never to recover. On the contrary, he continued his fall. If it had not been a matter of life and death, I would say that the scene before me was picturesque. The glow of the setting sun was reflected on my opponent's canopy as the green and brown camouflaged aircraft plunged straight down towards the sea. I waited in vain for the pilot to take to his parachute. Despite the shadows, I could still see a glow inside the cabin. I think the machine caught fire from the inside, probably when the oxygen cylinder was hit. Falling like a stone, the Spitfire finally plunged into the blue-green mirrorlike surface of the sea in a geyser of foam and spray. It was 17:20.

Wick too had spotted the Spitfires and climbed hard before pouncing on them from a favorable attack position. In a diving attack, Wick shot down Pilot Officer Paul A. Baillon of 609 Sqn. Polish pilot Zygmunt Klein then claimed hits on Wick's Messerschmitt, as did P.O. Eric Marrs. The attack disintegrated into a melee. Another JG 2 pilot, Rudolf Pflanz, saw a Spitfire shoot down a Bf 109, whose pilot bailed out. It was in fact Wick, who had jettisoned his canopy and jumped over the side of his Messerschmitt. Shot down by Flt. Lt. John Dundas, the solitary parachute drifted down towards the sea southwest of the Needles and disappeared without trace in the English Channel. It was a tough blow for the morale of the Reich's airmen and for Göring, who had made Wick the archetypal Tagjäger. Wick had progressed from Staffelkapitän to Kommodore of the Richthofen in only a matter of months. Having claimed some 30 victories during the summer of 1940 and received the Oak Leaves from Hitler himself on October 8, 1940, Wick was shot down barely two months after being appointed CO. Having given interviews in the American press that came across as arrogant and dismissive of the qualities of RAF fighter pilots, he certainly paid for his hubris. "I want to die shooting down RAF pilots," he had been quoted as saying.

By mid-December, calm had returned to the English Channel, at least by day. The month saw two unusual awards. On December 14, Major Joachim Schlichting (Kommandeur of III./JG 27), captured on September 6, was awarded the Knight's Cross even though he had only eight victories (five of which were in Spain). On the 30th, the Kommodore of JG 53, Major Günther Freiherr von Maltzahn received the same decoration with only 12 victories to his credit. These two Knight's Crosses were once again intended to honor these officers for the good conduct of their units.

In hindsight, it is perhaps clear that the Battle of Britain was not the close-run thing of British propaganda. Even today the battle is regarded as decisive. However, there were few serious preparations for a German landing even if such a scenario was possible. In reality, the Battle of Britain was the continuation of the air battles of May/June 1940 and comparing the losses of the two campaigns, it is clear that the French campaign was the most brutal and bloody. The campaign in the West saw three countries overrun by the Wehrmacht; the following months over England saw combat between two well-balanced aerial adversaries slugging it out against a highly politicized background.

From the outset of the battle, the Luftwaffe was confronted with problems. It was accepted that they would be disadvantaged by meteorology, insufficient intelligence, the entry into action of a coordinated air defense system including radar and the limits of the fighters' range. Weather played a role—sorties were often hampered by its vagaries. With the prevailing winds coming from the west, bombers and fighters encountered cloudbanks that were not always forecast and formation rendezvous points were constantly disrupted. Unsurprisingly then, the average *Jagdflieger* flew no more than 50 sorties during an 85-day period from August 8 to October 31. Contact with the enemy (*Feindberührung*) was made

In late November JG 53 returned their 500th victory and to celebrate this event, the aces of the Geschwader assembled for a photograph (probably in Etaples). From left: Lt. Ernst Klager, Oblt. Kurt Brändle, Hptm. Wolf-Dietrich Wilcke, Maj. Günther Freiherr von Maltzahn, Hptm. Heinz Bretnütz (with Knight's Cross), Ofw. Stefan Litjens, Hptm. Hans-Heinrich Brustellin, Lt. Erich Schmidt, and Oblt. Franz Götz.

Kommodore of JG 53, Maj. Günther Freiherr von Maltzahn. Having been stationed on the English Channel for several months, JG 53 returned to Germany at the end of 1940.

on only around 20 of these. For around 20 days at the height of the battle there were no German aircraft at all in the skies over England. When the bombers turned on London in September, the 1,000 Luftwaffe aircraft of the British "official" history were never more than 400. On only two occasions (September 7 and 15) could the Luftwaffe put more than 300 bombers in the air and for nearly 20 days of the battle the Luftwaffe flew fewer than 200 sorties.

On October 16, 1940, Siegfried Bethke of JG 2 reflected on the general situation in his diary. He realized that destroying the RAF in a few days, as Göring was still claiming, was a fool's dream: "The English seem to be putting up with things quite well. Important things did not happen."

Bethke was lucky—he would survive the war unscathed. Ulrich Steinhilper survived too; mentally and physically exhausted, he was shot down over England in late October and entered captivity.

While German losses during the battle remained "bearable" (some 140% of those of the RAF) for an attacker facing a structured defense, over the UK losses were of course "permanent." The Tagjäger suffered notable attrition, losing a number of experienced Condor Legion veterans (Mayer, von Houwald, Harder) but also talented young pilots with a handful of victories gleaned with difficulty in the *Westfeldzug*.

During the Battle of Britain, 25 Knight's Crosses were awarded. Three of these were only on an honorary basis while five of the recent recipients were lost over England in a short period of time (two taken captive). As to the validity of German claims during the battle, Hptm. Erich von Selle of II./JG 3 responded to an official request on the credit to be given to a rather effusive victory report: "Given the conditions of combat over England, in the majority of cases, there is no witness who can confirm or refute the statements. However, there is no reason to contradict this report."

On December 24, Hitler arrived on the Channel coast to spend Christmas with soldiers and airmen stationed on the English Channel. He is welcomed here in Desvres by Maj. Günther Lützow, leading JG 3.

Waiting for *Barbarossa*, 1941

With the return of spring and better weather, the Jagdgeschwader resumed the fight against Britain. However, combat was constrained by the forthcoming campaign in the East. Sporadic fighting took place either to counter the intrusions of Blenheim or RAF reconnaissance Spitfires or during free-hunt incursions into English airspace. At that time, some Gruppen were converting onto and operating the new Bf 109 variant, the F type (Friedrich), which gave them a certain qualitative advantage. The "Friedrich" presented a number of enhancements over the successive improvements introduced to the venerable "Emil" with which the Jagdwaffe had gone to war over Poland.

The basic airframe had undergone a redesign with the aim of improving aerodynamic efficiency—especially in the area of the wing and tailplane. Both spinner and wingtips were rounded and more streamlined and the Emil's horizontal stabilizer brace supports had been eliminated. In addition, the tailwheel was now fully retractable. However the Friedrich did not feature wing armament and weight of fire was thus reduced in comparison to the older sub-type—although the engine-mounted cannon and the cowl machine guns being aligned along the "axis of flight" made aiming easier. There were also some structural issues with early examples, a number of pilots being lost after tearing the wings off in high-G maneuvers.

In March 1941, there were some 40 Tagjagd claims (not all of them certified). Confirmed aces, such as Ihlefeld and Bretnütz, increased their scores while younger pilots, such as Walter Hoeckner and Paul Stolte, opened theirs.

Walter Oesau received the Oak Leaves for his 40th victory on February 6, 1941, as did Joppien on April 23. Young Oblt. Hans-Ekkehard Bob (9./JG 54) was awarded the Knight's Cross on March 7 for his 19 *Luftsiege*.

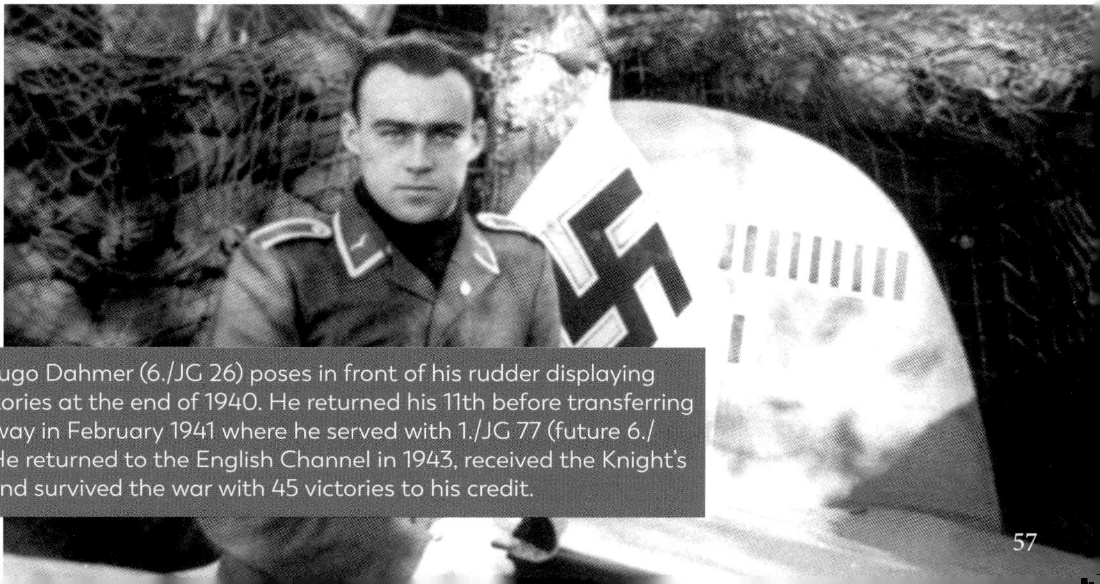

Uffz. Hugo Dahmer (6./JG 26) poses in front of his rudder displaying ten victories at the end of 1940. He returned his 11th before transferring to Norway in February 1941 where he served with 1./JG 77 (future 6./JG 5). He returned to the English Channel in 1943, received the Knight's Cross and survived the war with 45 victories to his credit.

Bf 109 Friedrich of JG 53. For much of 1941, a detachment of JG 53 remained in the Netherlands to support JG 1. The first variants of the Friedrich appeared in late 1940 and by early 1941 the F-2 was being delivered. By May 1941 production of the F-4 started and the variant entered service in June 1941. The Bf 109 F-4 was the upgraded variant of the Friedrich powered by the new DB 601 E. For the RAF and by way of comparison, the Spitfire V entered service in February 1941 (one squadron) and a further four squadrons in May were equipped with the type.

One of the new Friedrichs. Bf 109 F-2 White 12 of Lt. Karl Vockelmann, 7./JG 53, spring 1941. Posted missing in action on May 19, 1943, he was credited with nine victories.

In February 1941 a new Kommodore was appointed to succeed Helmut Wick at the head of JG 2. Hptm. Wilhelm Balthasar was an ace who at the time enjoyed almost as large a reputation as Wick's, having been one of the leading Luftwaffe fighter pilots through 1940.

Official portrait of Wilhelm Balthasar to mark his winning the Knight's Cross.

On April 7, 1941 Oblt. Hubert Mütherich leading 5./JG 54 shot down two Yugoslav Blenheims as seen here painted on his rudder scoreboard beneath a row of victories over RAF machines returned while flying with I./JG 77.

Life in the West had become almost routine when, at the end of March, II. and III./JG 77 as well as I./LG 2 were urgently withdrawn to fight in the Balkans. Shortly afterwards, in stages, most of the JGs returned to the Reich to receive new aircraft.

The Balkans: *Marita* and *Merkur*

In March, the Serbs overthrew the existing regime and refused passage to the Italian-German troops attacking Greece. This forced the Reich to engage additional units and, on April 6, 1941, Operation *Marita*, the joint invasion of Yugoslavia and Greece, opened. Jagdgeschwader 27, 54, and 77 were deployed to the Balkans, but their opponents, flying mostly obsolete aircraft, were swept away in a few days. On April 6, two I./LG 2 pilots, Lt. Fritz Geisshardt and Oblt. Erwin Clausen, shared seven Yugoslav Fury biplanes. German losses were mainly due to poor conditions of local airfields. However, Knight's Cross bearer Herbert Ihlefeld, leading I./LG 2, was shot down near Nisch on the first day of the fighting. Captured by Serbian soldiers, he was maltreated, threatened with execution and only owed his salvation to the arrival of German forces.

On the 23rd, Hptm. Franz-Heinz Lange, Kommandeur of II./JG 77, with two victories, was shot down and killed in Koropion. Two more future JG 77 *Experten,* Lt. Siegfried Freytag and Oblt. Erich Friedrich, also victims of anti-aircraft fire, would be captured and released at the end of April.

Over Greece, the Tagjagd encountered the tough RAF Hurricanes. On April 15, Oblt. Gustav Rödel (4./JG 27) claimed a Hurricane and two Greek PZL 24s; on April 19, Fw. Reinhold Schmetzer and Oblt. Kurt Ubben (8./JG 77) were credited with three Blenheims and two Hurricanes respectively. The particularity of *Marita* would be the massive return to

Herbert Ihlefeld, with a bandaged head, returns to his unit, I./LG 2, after having been rescued by a German advance unit.

Lt. Emil Omert in the cockpit of a Bf 109 *Jabo* at Molaoi airfield (Peloponnese) during the Greek campaign. Note the Richthofen badge, evidently a machine acquired from JG 2.

Jabo operations. As in England six months earlier, pilots of some Staffeln (such as 7./JG 77) with experience in dive-bombing, mounted attacks on shipping evacuating British troops. In the absence of any aerial victories, these actions were often taken into account in the ranking of aces. Staffelkapitän 7./JG 77 Oblt. Huy enjoyed notable success during JG 77's anti-shipping sorties. Flying out of Larissa—facilities were rudimentary with 250-kg bombs loaded manually—he hit a 20,000-ton troop transport on 27 April.

Marita, the new *blitzkrieg*, ended on April 29. But, while few Wehrmacht soldiers were killed, some fighter Gruppen were reduced to just a handful of airworthy machines.

Hitler sent another "message of peace" to Britain, which was met with another rebuttal. The Germans thus decided to launch Operation *Merkur*, the airborne invasion of Crete, the last of Continental Europe held by opposing forces. To support this operation, only II. and III. /JG 77 with I./LG 2 were installed in the Peloponnese. *Merkur* opened on May 20. The Tagjagd did not stand out at the beginning of the invasion because, warned by Ultra, the enemy evacuated its planes to Egypt. However, the *Jabos* were active against the Royal Navy. When the RAF sent its light bombers to the island at the end of the campaign, a number of Blenheims were downed by Lt. Omert, Hptm. Ihlefeld, Oblt. Hoeckner, and Lt. Geisshardt, all confirmed aces or aces in the making. But, in return, II./JG 77 lost its Kommandeur, Hptm. Helmut Henz. A former "Spaniard" with four victories, he had notched up a further three before falling victim over the Aegean Sea to a Blenheim's defensive fire.

On May 30, as *Merkur* ended with the fall of Crete, Luftwaffe units hastened northward to prepare for *Barbarossa*.

On May 14, 1941, Lt. Diethelm von Eichel-Streiber returned to Molaoi despite a direct hit from anti-aircraft fire over Crete that shredded his rudder. He ended the war with 96 victories and the Knight's Cross.

Molaoi, Greece. Emils of III./JG 77 still displaying the JG 2 Richthofen badge.

Over Malta

As part of the aid package to Italy, the Luftwaffe sent a fighter Staffel, 7./JG 26, to Sicily, led by the recent Knight's Cross bearer, Oblt. Joachim Müncheberg. On February 12, 1941, the first operation targeted Malta: three Hurricanes were claimed. 7./JG 26 would operate in the Mediterranean until September. On April 6, the Staffel rapidly intervened in Yugoslavia, Müncheberg shooting down three aircraft and Oblt. Klaus Mietusch a fourth. In June, Müncheberg's small "troop" arrived on the African continent in support of JG 27.

After six months of combat, the results returned by this single Staffel were impressive. No losses were recorded, while 42 victories were claimed (half by Müncheberg alone, the rest

Fitting a 250-kg bomb to the belly rack of a JG 77 Bf 109.

On May 20, 1941 (D-Day of *Merkur*), 5./JG 77 lost Obfw. Werner Petermann who was forced to land his Bf 109 on a beach in Crete. This former Kriegsmarine veteran had nine victories to his credit (including two Yugoslav Me 109s). He returned from his Australian captivity in 1947.

Kommandeur III./JG 27 Hptm. Max Dobislav in his Black 5, a Bf 109 E-7 of 8./JG 27 (W.Nr. 5578) about to depart on a sortie against Malta, from Gela, Sicily, loaded with a 250-kg bomb. Dobislav returned his ninth victory, a Hurricane, on May 15 over Malta.

being divided between various aces including Mietusch and Lt. Hans Johannsen). According to Caldwell, the intervention of these fighters in this brand-new theater disrupted British plans and forced local commanders to drastically review their strategy.

Following the end of the Balkans campaign, III./JG 27 flew from Greece to Sicily to reinforce X. Fliegerkorps assaulting Malta and, more specifically, Müncheberg's Staffel. Their first sorties were flown from Gela—a field strip on Sicily's south coast—on May 6, 1941. For no losses, five victories were claimed, four of them by Oblt. Erbo von Kageneck, leading 7. Staffel. By the end of May, they had already departed Sicily for Germany to prepare for *Barbarossa*.

Although this six-month period was decisive, both politically and strategically, the Tagjagd was forced to engage its forces piecemeal. In the Balkans, the German aces' opponents were no match for them. It was therefore only a transitional period that allowed some aces to boost their scorecards, often more easily than the previous year.

Hptm. Müncheberg at the controls of his 7./JG 26 Emil White 12 on Sicily during his successful period operating over Malta. He returned nearly half of the Staffel's victories over Malta and was awarded the Oak Leaves on May 7, 1941. Note the Staffelkapitän's pennant on the aerial mast and a gun camera in the wing leading edge.

Joachim Müncheberg at Gela with the German actress Carola Höhn, who was visiting the German fighter pilots. Müncheberg courted her assiduously but she would marry another Knight's Cross bearer, Arved Crüger (from KG 30).

Müncheberg, Johanson and Ofw. Ernst Laube of 7./JG 26 on Sicily. Laube returned two victories over Malta. He was appointed Kommandeur I./JG 3 in mid-1944 and led IV./JG 4 in the defense of the Reich. He survived the war with around 20 victories.

Sicily, May 1941. Oblt. Erbo Graf von Kageneck preparing for a sortie over Malta in his Bf 109.

This Bf 109 Friedrich of JG 54 seen on June 22, 1941 at a Soviet airfield well illustrates the first days of *Barbarossa*. In the foreground is a Polikarpov I-16 fighter that the Luftwaffe had already faced in Spain. VVS (Soviet Air Forces) equipment was largely obsolete but would soon be updated and modernized.

Barbarossa, 1941

On June 22, 1941, the Wehrmacht invaded the USSR. To face the Soviet giant, the Tagjagd committed some 20 fighter Gruppen, or 793 Bf 109s, of which 619 were serviceable. The numbers were comparatively small but the fighters were supported, in the north, by the small but vigorous Finnish air arm and in the south by Romanian and Slovak elements with outdated equipment.

Opposite them, the VVS, the Soviet Air Forces, was beginning to modernize. Rows of obsolete aircraft were lined up on airfields next to the new Yak and MiG fighters that had just left the factories. On the first day of *Barbarossa*, no fewer than 1,800 Soviet aircraft were destroyed. The Luftwaffe claimed 1,811 victories on this day (1,489 on the ground and 322 in the air). There were many multiple claims: in JG 51, Oblt. Hohagen returned three as did Ofw. Walter Gasthaus and Oblt. Franz Hahn, while Oblt. Karl-Gottfried Nordmann claimed four. It was a similar story in the other JGs. But this did not mean that the enemy was crushed: despite massive losses, the VVS could still commit aircraft.

Kommodore JG 54 Hannes Trautloft noted in his diary:

> Shortly before 03:00 on 22 June, the three Gruppen of JG 54 were airborne from their respective airfields with the mission of supporting Army Group North: supporting the Panzer and the Heer [divisions], escorting Ju 88 bombers from KG 1, 76, and 77, and also destroying bridges. The aerodromes of Gerlinden

> and Lindental reported the overflight of enemy bombers. The standby Staffel got airborne to prevent them from reaching East Prussia. Of the 22 SB-2 "Martins," 17 were shot down. The others managed to evade this fate. Everywhere there were planes plunging earthwards in flames, the skies filled with parachutes.

For its first day of combat in the USSR, JG 54 claimed 45 victories, including four for the Staffelkapitän 1./JG 54, Oblt. Adolf Kinzinger, to take his total to 12, and two returned by I. Gruppe's Spain veteran Hptm. Reinhard Seiler. Future Knight's Cross bearer Uffz. Fritz Tegtmeier returned his first. The next day, Kommodore Trautloft wrote in his journal: "We are feeling the effects of the first day, our fatigue is enormous. It was only after midnight that we finally got some rest. Two hours later, we are up, ready to participate in the first sorties of the day."

The first day of the invasion cost the lives of two Knight's Cross bearers. Maj. Wolfgang Schellmann, leading JG 27, returned his last victory downing a biplane before being brought down himself. At the bridge over the Niemen at Vishvill being used by the LVI Panzer Corps, Hptm. Heinz Bretnütz, Kommandeur of II./JG 53—top of the Geschwader victory list and the tenth-highest-scoring Luftwaffe ace at that time—was also shot down by the defensive fire of a Soviet SB-2, having just returned his 32nd victory. With his engine hit and seriously wounded in the left leg, he glided down for a crash-landing in his Bf 109 F-2 "Chevron Triangle" (W.Nr. 6674). With difficulty he hauled himself out of the cockpit, applied a rudimentary bandage to his leg, and stumbled away from the scene to hole up for the night. The following day he continued to move southwest and was eventually found by a Lithuanian forrester sympathetic to the Germans. He was back in German lines two days later. But it was too late: his leg wound was infected and he died during the amputation. The loss of these two Spain veterans was an ominous portent for the Luftwaffe. Bretnütz was replaced as Kommandeur by Hptm. Walter Spies, also a Spain veteran, who had flown Hs 126s in the West before converting to fighters during 1941. He returned his first two victories on June 22, while future ace Uffz. Herbert Rollwage of 4./JG 53 was credited with his first.

On June 23, to slow the German advance, the Red Army launched three attacks that day with light bomber formations: one in the morning, the second at noon, and the third in the evening. Thirty SB-2 and DB-3 bombers were claimed and about 65 the next day.

On 23 June at 11:00, Oblt. Hans-Ekkehard Bob, of 9./JG 54, took off from Blumenfeld to lead two Schwärme in the area of Kaunas, Lithuania. They soon intercepted the first of some 27 SB-2 twin-engine bombers of which 13 were claimed. During the attack, Bob's Bf 109 was hit by an SB-2 gunner:

This pilot proudly paints on his rudder a new victory bar adorned with a red star.

Seen here during the *Westfeldzug*, the campaign in the West, Knight's Cross bearer Wolfgang Schellmann (with map), commanding JG 27, was killed on the first day of the invasion after bailing out behind Soviet lines.

> My 109 began to vibrate, then to pitch as if it had become a wounded beast. I immediately broke off and turned onto a southerly heading. As I was flying low and I was about 200 kilometers away from the German lines, anxiety started to grow and then increased tenfold when the engine stopped dead. I had no alternative but to land, but under my wings was nothing but an immense wooded area. By chance I saw a little clearing. Gear up, I put down my Yellow 1, which slid along the grass on its belly for several meters before coming to a stop. I clambered out of the cockpit, expecting to be fired on at any moment but all was calm. I spotted the survival kit that had been thrown from the machine on impact—it comprised a bag containing a piece of bread (hard and dry), a few pharmaceutical products, and two bottles filled with tea. With the summer heat (40°), this liquid was essential. I grabbed it and immediately set off into the woods, since I could already hear the voices of men and the howling of dogs. I had to put as much distance as possible between my pursuers and myself.

Later that afternoon Bob heard the powerful noise of several Messerschmitts—escort for a search-and-rescue Storch—but chose to stay in his hideout to await nightfall. Under the cover of darkness, he began a long march to the west carefully avoiding roads, bridges, and settlements for fear of Soviet patrols. After three days—his face blistered by mosquito bites—he managed to rejoin his lines.

The invasion of the USSR generated a proliferation of aces in the Luftwaffe fighter arm. Many young German pilots claiming these *Luftsiege* went on to "enjoy" meteoric careers. On

Bf 109 Friedrich Yellow 1 belly-landed by Oblt. Hans-Ekkehard Bob, of 9./ JG 54

Austrian Oblt. Kurt Sochatzy, Staffelkapitän of 7./JG 3, in front of his Bf 109 F shortly before the launch of *Barbarossa*. His machine was named after his wife. On August 3, 1941, he collided with his 38th victim and had to bail out near Kiev. He entered captivity from which he returned in 1947. The Knight's Cross would be awarded to him nine days after he was reported missing.

June 22, 1941, Lt. Karl Bergmann of 3./JG 3 returned his first victory. On July 11, he already had 12 before being shot down and wounded. On June 25, Lt. Gustav Langanke (5./JG 27) started his day with one victory to his credit. He closed it with eight.

On the afternoon of June 25, during a free-hunt sortie over the Balta/Jassy/Kishinew sector, Oblt. Walter Hoeckner of 6./JG 77 claimed eight SB-2s shot down. Faced with the rapid German advance, the VVS deployed everything it could. Large formations of light bombers were thus sent out to attack German columns seemingly without concern for casualties. At 10:40 on June 26, eight Bf 109s of III./JG 77 were scrambled against a formation of up to 60 SB-2 twins—20 were shot down in short order, four being claimed by Oblt. Ubben, taking his score to ten, and five by Ofw. Schmetzer. Lt. Emil Omert doubled his score with five victories (5–9). Future 8./JG 77 ace Fw. Albert Palm shot down an SB-2 for his second that afternoon.

There followed a plethora of claims: on one day alone, June 30, 1941, JG 51 was credited with over a hundred victories including five each for Mölders (who thus passed Richthofen's score), Joppien, and Bär, while Kommandeure Fözö (II. Gruppe) and Leppla (III.Gruppe) both passed twenty.

Bf 109 E Black 5 flown by Lt. Gustav Langanke of 5./JG 27.

During these first weeks in the USSR, there were a number of notable awards of the Knight's Cross. In general terms, however, the number of victories required was on the rise. On June 27, Herbert Ihlefeld, Kommandeur I./LG 2, received the Oak Leaves after his 40 victories. On July 5, Wolf-Dieter Huy (7./JG 77) received the Knight's Cross for nine victories, though he had sunk shipping during *Marita/Merkur*.

On the same day, July 5, Alexander von Winterfeldt, leading III./JG 77, received the Knight's Cross for his six victories, having been credited with four in 1918. Bernhard Woldenga, the Kommodore of JG 77, had no victories to his credit but was also awarded the Knight's Cross. These were the last Knight's Crosses awarded partially or entirely for the "good conduct of a unit." That there had been this honor was disproportionate. The Knight's

Claims for the Jagdgeschwader in the East, 22 June–30 September 1941

I./JG 3—273, II./JG 3—411, III./JG 3—367
I./JG 51—252, II./JG 51—321, III./JG 51—308, IV./JG 51—468
II./JG 52—248, III./JG 52—216
I./JG 53—200+, II./JG 53—194, III./JG 53—373
I./JG 54—212, II./JG 54—395, III./JG 54—223
II./JG 77—211, III./JG 77—374

A closer look at the claims of one Eastern Front Geschwader, JG 53, is revealing. The Stab and I./JG 53 only stayed in the East for six weeks. At first glance, their campaign seems to have been a simple military "walk in the park," with pilots moving from aerodrome to aerodrome while shooting down dozens of aircraft. But during this period, these two units lost 15 aircraft and three pilots killed, with one taken captive. A Kommandeur was among the missing and the Kommodore von Maltzahn had to make three forced landings himself. About 200 victories were claimed: the Kommodore, credited with his 16th victory on June 22, left the Eastern Front with 49 *Luftsiege*; Oblt. Hans-Joachim Heinecke, with no victories on June 22, finished the campaign with 16 *Abschüsse* and was appointed Staffelkapitän of I./JG 53.

These numbers are lower than those of III./JG 53, a Gruppe formed under the leadership of Werner Mölders and which produced a number of *Draufgänger* (go-getters). Detached from the rest of the unit, III./JG 53 operated over Army Group Center. At the end of its campaign in the East, on September 27, 1941, III./JG 53 had filed paperwork for no fewer than 373 victories. These claims were made for the loss of some 31 Friedrichs either seriously damaged or destroyed and just three pilots killed. One of these was Knight's Cross holder Lt. Erich Schmidt, (Knight's Cross awarded July 23 for 31 victories) who was downed by Soviet anti-aircraft fire near Dubno.

II./JG 53 (minus its 6. Staffel) remained in the northern sector. Despite the early loss of Kommandeur Bretnütz, over 14 weeks and for the loss of six pilots, the Gruppe returned some 194 victories.

On July 15, 1941, Hptm. Walter Oesau (III./JG 3) was awarded the Swords to the Knight's Cross (after Mölders and Galland) for his 80 victories. He then left the Eastern Front to take command of JG 2 in the West.

Kommandeur I./JG 53 Franz von Werra would be credited with 13 victories in the East but left Russia in mid-August 1941 to get married. In the deckchair at right, his Bf 109 F is in the background.

Von Werra.

Lt. Winfried Schmidt (right) with his Kapitän, Oblt. Willi Stange. An ace with 12 victories, Stange was captured and executed on June 22, 1941.

July 5, 1941, shortly after the opening of *Barbarossa*, General Kurt Pflugbeil (back to camera) visited JG 77 at Jassy, Romania. To his left, Hpt. Ihlefeld (I./LG 2) looks on as the Kommodore presents Oblt. Huy (partially masked) with his Knight's Cross. To the right of the general, Lt. Emil Omert looks on.

Cross would henceforth only be awarded to combatants on the front line. Oblt. Wolf-Dieter Huy's award on the other hand could be directly attributed to his successes in the Balkans and Crete.

JG 77 received three more during the course of 1941: Fw. Rudolf Schmidt on August 30 for 27 victories, Oblt. Kurt Ubben on September 4 for 28 victories, and Oblt. Heinrich Setz on December 31, 1941 for 45 victories. More JG 77 pilots had opened and progressed their accounts by this stage. In II./JG 77 Uffz. Ernst-Wilhelm Reinert returned his first victory on August 8 and finished the year with 24, while Oblt. Anton Hackl had achieved 26 victories by the end of 1941. In III./JG 77 Hptm. Ubben was appointed Kommandeur on September 5, 1941 and had reached 61 victories by December 31, 1941, while Lt. Emil Omert had 39, with Fw. Georg Seckel on 27, and Wolf-Dieter Huy on thirty.

Future Knight's Cross winner Uffz. Eduard Isken (7./JG 77) recalled the early victories in the East:

> As Staffelkapitän Huy's usual wingman, I saw him return victories, but I never had any opportunities to score myself. The sky seemed to empty as I got there. One day, Huy gave me my chance. Soviet columns had been attacked by Stukas for whom we were providing top cover. Russian fighters appeared. Huy shot down two of them, pulled away, then left me the third. I got in behind the Russian biplane but then a stoppage occurred

Oblt. Huy contemplates the rudder of his Friedrich after the award of the Knight's Cross. He claimed a limited number of aerial kills but sank a number of ships during *Jabo* actions in the Balkans.

> in my onboard armament. This was often a problem in Russia. Was it due to my *Waffenwart* [armorer] or the devil? I'll never know! My victory list would otherwise almost certainly have been longer. However, I did of course eventually get off the mark.

On July 16, Hermann Staiger received the Knight's Cross for 26 victories. On July 30, Robert Olejnik, Staffelkapitän 1./JG 3, was awarded the Knight's Cross, by which time he had 32 *Abschüsse*. According to his own account, Olejnik shot down a Russian I-16 fighter at 03:40 on June 22, 1941, the first pilot to score a victory over the Eastern Front. He shot down four Russian bombers on June 23, to record his seventh through tenth victories, and a further five on June 26 (11–15).

Toward the end of the year, on November 17, Edmund Wagner was posthumously awarded the Knight's Cross for his 57 victories. On December 18, Gerhard Köppen became a Knight's Cross bearer with 45 victories and, on December 20, Reinhard Seiler had 43 *Luftsiege* (added to his nine from Spain) before finally being awarded the decoration. While acknowledging that many Russian aircraft were often obsolete, it was also the case that "Red" pilots had fought in Spain and, in 1939, even "rubbed shoulders" with the Japanese in Manchuria. Like the Germans, they therefore had modern air combat experience.

Once again, the Luftwaffe sustained losses in the face of enemy numerical superiority and lost quality pilots, on occasion Knight's Cross bearers. On June 24, the Kommandeur of I./JG 53, Oblt. Wilfried Balfanz (ten victories), disappeared in a fight with SB-3s in Pruszana. Two days later, Hptm. Lothar Keller, leading II./JG 3, collided with an Fi 156 Storch during a reconnaissance mission near Stojanow. Keller, a former member of the Condor Legion, would receive the Knight's Cross posthumously for his 23 victories (including three in Spain).

On August 25, Hptm. Hermann-Friedrich Joppien, Kommandeur of I./JG 51, hit the ground near Bryansk in the middle of a battle after winning his 70th and final victory. A favorite of German propaganda, Joppien's profile was as high as that of Mölders and Wick but, today, his name is more or less forgotten.

On August 31, Oblt. Erich Schmidt (9./JG 53), hit by anti-aircraft fire, jumped clear over enemy lines at Dubno and was reported missing. Having won his first victory in France, he had 19 *Luftsiege* to his credit at the end of 1940 and 47 at the time of his death.

On July 30, Robert Olejnik was awarded the Knight's Cross, by which time he had returned 32 *Abschüsse*. Although a Knight's Cross is visible around his neck in the photo series from which this image is taken, the rudder of his Bf 109 F-2 White 7 only shows 21 victories.

Crash-landed Bf 109 Emil Red 5 of 8./JG 77 flown by Ofw. Reinhold Schmetzer. According to one veteran and contrary to the official account, Schmetzer's Emil was forced down after a collision with the machine flown by Reinhard Heydrich.

In Profile:

SS-Gruppenführer Reinhard Heydrich in JG 77

During the course of July 1941, Hptm. Anton Mader, Kommandeur of II./JG 77, was assigned a rather "awkward" new pilot: SS-Gruppenführer Reinhard Heydrich, infamous head of the Sicherheitsdienst (SD) and of the Reichssicherheitshauptamt (RSHA), one of the most powerful men in the Nazi hierarchy. A keen pilot, Heydrich had already flown combat sorties with II./JG 77 in Norway in his personal Emil. Flying from Balta on July 22, 1941, his machine was badly damaged over Yampol by Soviet anti-aircraft fire. He managed to crash-land in no-man's land, and was missing for the best part of two days before running into a German patrol. His wife Lina described the incident: "Reinhard comes home, dirty, unshaven and very upset … He landed behind enemy lines, had hidden for two days and two nights and made his way on foot back to German units."

Heydrich was awarded the silver bar for combat missions and the Iron Cross 1st class. According to one account, Hitler noticed the new decorations and, apparently horrified at the thought of his Security Chief being captured by the Russians, strictly forbade any further combat flying. Luftwaffe Reserve "Major" Heydrich was grounded, much to the relief, one imagines, of Kommandeur Mader. The number of missions flown by Heydrich is not known but the Frontflugspange (Front Flying Clasp) in Silver was usually given for 60 combat missions.

Heydrich had flown briefly with II./JG 77 in Norway during Operation *Weserübung*, in the uniform of a Luftwaffe Hauptmann before joining 6. Staffel commanded by Hptm. Franz-Heinz Lange.

On August 1, 1941, near Mogilew, General Bruno Loerzer (center) presented the Knight's Cross to Oblt. Karl-Heinz Schnell (left), leading 8./JG 51 (31 victories), and Karl-Gottfried Nordmann, Kommandeur IV./JG 51 (31 victories). These two Knight's Cross bearers would survive the war.

On September 7, Oblt. Erich Hohagen (5./JG 51) had to abandon his aircraft in combat. Seriously wounded, he received the Knight's Cross for his 31 victories but did not return to the front until a year later.

On September 9, Oblt. Hubert Mütherich (5./JG 54) was brought down by MiGs near Krasnoje Selo; he attempted to land but struck a tree. He had received the Knight's Cross the previous month for his 31 victories (43 at the time of his death).

On 3 October, Obfw. Heinrich Hoffmann (12./JG 51) did not return after a clash with IL-2s near Jelnja. He had 63 victories to his credit (one in the West). A Knight's Cross holder, he would be awarded the Oak Leaves, the first non-commissioned officer to receive the award but also the first Wehrmacht soldier to receive them posthumously. On October 8, Oblt. Kurt Lasse, leading 9./JG 77, hit his wingman over Perekop. He had 39 victories (one in the West). He would be awarded the Knight's Cross posthumously.

On November 17, Obfw. Edmund Wagner (9./JG 51) was lost in a battle with bombers near Pafmutovka. He had won a single victory over England, adding a further 56 in the East. As a young ace he had a meteoric career. He was awarded the Knight's Cross posthumously.

Staffelkapitän 8./ JG 77, Oblt. Kurt Ubben (light shirt, blowing his nose) was awarded the Knight's Cross on September 4, 1941 for 28 victories.

Kommodore Mölders presides over the funeral of Oblt. Hans Kolbow, Staka 5./JG 51. Kolbow, a former fighter pilot in Spain (no victories), returned 27 *Luftsiege* (13 of them in the West) including eight during the Battle of Britain. He shot down five Soviet bombers on June 25. On July 16, 1941, hit by anti-aircraft fire near Stara Bychow, he safely evacuated his Bf 109 F "Red 1," but his parachute failed to deploy. He received the Knight's Cross posthumously.

The most notable loss, indirectly linked to the Eastern Front, would be that of Werner Mölders. Leading JG 51, he had continued to carve out his reputation in the East. On June 22, 1941, he received the Swords to the Knight's Cross for his 72 victories before being the first Wehrmacht soldier to be awarded the Diamonds to the Knight's Cross after 101 *Luftsiege*. He was the first fighter ace to reach the symbolic 100 mark, and was then grounded with a *Flugverbot* (flight ban) being imposed before taking up the role of Inspector of Fighters in Berlin. Mölders, however, took advantage of his duties to visit his comrades in the East. He would "borrow" aircraft to try out new tactics, scoring some additional victories that he would allow his temporary wingmen to claim, in order to maintain secrecy on these flights. On November 22, 1941, Oberst Mölders boarded an He 111 to attend Ernst Udet's funeral in Berlin. The twin-engine machine crashed in bad weather. Two days after his death, JG 51 received the *Ehrenname* (honor title) Jagdgeschwader Mölders, the only Luftwaffe ace to have a fighter Geschwader named after him.

At the beginning of December, the harsh Russian winter stopped the Wehrmacht at the gates of Moscow and fighting in the air tailed off. However, despite their successes, German pilots faced surprisingly strong resistance from their Soviet counterparts. Contrary to the general opinion prevailing on June 22, the Stalinist regime did not collapse after five months of fierce fighting. On the ground, as had been the case with Napoleon's armies a century earlier, the tactics of scorched earth were ruthlessly applied. The submission of the Soviet people to their "red tsar" changed the course of the Second World War.

On August 6, 1941, Oblt. Hubert Mütherich (left) (31 victories), leading 5./JG 54, received the Knight's Cross at the same time as his comrade, the Austrian Lt. Josef Pöhs (right) (28 victories). On September 9, Mütherich was killed near Leningrad.

Four notable aces, from left: Mütherich, Philipp, Hrabak and Pöhs. Only Hrabak (125 victories) survived the war.

Bf 109 F-4 (W.Nr. 7134) with close-up of the rudder and victory tally of Hptm. Herbert Ihlefeld, then Gruppenkommandeur of I.(J)/LG 2 or, if taken in 1942, I./JG 77. The rudder represents Ihlefeld's score as it stood on July 12, 1941, when I.(J)/LG 2 was still exclusively equipped with the Bf 109 E. The score appears identical to the well-known and often-published rudder of Ihlefeld's Bf 109 E-7 (W.Nr. 6095).

Wintergerst welcomed with flowers, possibly replaying for the cameras the events of August 12, 1941.

The Strange Odyssey of Two Aces in the Crimea

Eugen Wintergerst was born in Lauben on June 13, 1915 into a peasant family and joined the army in 1938 with the aim of moving to the Luftwaffe. He began training in 1939 and joined 4./JG 77 shortly before *Barbarossa*. Like many other aces, he scored freely during the early stages of the invasion. On August 11, he was credited with his sixth and seventh victories after downing two SB-2 bombers—just 24 hours later his tally was fourteen. That day, Obfw. Wintergerst took off from Zebrikowo to test a machine, wearing just his bathing trunks. He had barely got airborne when he sighted a formation of nine SB-3 bombers intent on raiding the airfield. He immediately lined up for a series of passes, knocking down seven of the Soviet bombers in quick succession. Hptm. Mader arrived on the scene just in time to witness the fires on the ground from the impacts. Wintergerst returned to base waggling his wings over the airstrip. The ground crews ran to greet him, but they were by no means the only ones: a visiting general was among them. Embarrassed by his inappropriate dress, Wintergerst was unwilling to climb out of the cockpit in front of the superior officer. But the general was happy to turn a blind eye.

On September 24, 1941, his luck ended. Wintergerst had returned some 20 victories. Over the Crimea, he collided with a comrade, the Austrian Lt. Herwig Zuzic (13 victories). Both aces jumped clear and were captured. Facing a political commissar, they pretended to be deserters who had abandoned their machines. Convinced, the man handed them over to higher authority. They were made to sign insulting propaganda targeting Hitler, with leaflets dropped over the German lines. For the Soviets this was enough to compromise the two. They were then trained as saboteurs and, a few weeks later, parachuted into Romania, where they quickly handed themselves in; the two comrades were soon posted back to the West joining I./JG 2 and then, in 1943, moving to 9./JG 1. Their destiny would remain surprisingly linked. Zuzic, leading the Staffel, was killed near Zuidzande, Netherlands, on August 19, 1943 in a collision. Wintergerst, promoted to officer, succeeded him at the head of 9. Staffel but was killed on September 4, 1943 near Berck, France, in a dogfight with Spitfires. He managed to bail out but his parachute failed to deploy. He had added two victories to his scoreboard, including a B-17 *Viermot* (four-engined bomber).

Pilots of I./JG 2 take in the sun at Marignane, Marseille, late 1942. From left: Lt. Wintergerst, Oblt. Zuzic, Oblt. Fritz Edelmann, and Oblt. Elmar Resch.

Africa, 1941

On February 12, 1941, General Erwin Rommel arrived in Tripoli to protect the Italian possession of Libya threatened by a British counteroffensive from Egypt—following an attack by Mussolini's weakened army. The ambitious Rommel then exceeded the Führer's instructions and turned his mission into an offensive action, taking advantage of the deployment of British troops from Egypt to Greece. However, the war in the desert was a supply-based conflict. When one of the belligerents made territorial gains, logistics had to follow.

To support his expeditionary force—the Deutsches Afrika Korps (DAK)—the Luftwaffe provided a reconnaissance squadron and a heavy fighter group. At Rommel's request, on April 15, 1941, the first elements of 1. and 2. Staffel JG 27 began relocating to North Africa, flying into Ain el Gazala airfield, west of Tobruk, between April 18 and 24. I./JG 27 would go down in history as the first single-engine fighter unit to support the DAK, after a somewhat limited participation in *Marita*, the Balkans operation. As it happened, the emblem of I./JG 27 was a map of Africa with an African's head and a leopard's head superimposed. However, this emblem dated back to the origins of the unit and to its first Kommandeur, Hptm. Helmut Riegel, who was apparently nostalgic for the lost colonies.

On April 19, 1941, 1./JG 27 was in action over Tobruk, returning four victories; two were attributed to Oblt. Wolfgang Redlich, an ace of the unit. A future great—the second "Star of Africa"—Lt. Werner Schröer was credited with his first aerial victory, an RAF Hurricane of 274 Sqn shot down near Tobruk. In this encounter, Schröer was forced to belly-land his Bf 109 E-7 (W.Nr. 3790) at Ain el Gazala. On the 21st, the young Obfw. Albert Espenlaub, a gliding fanatic, returned his first victory. On the 23rd, among other claims, came one from an Ofhr. Hans-Joachim Marseille.

A Rotte of I./JG 27 over the desert.

Kommandeur I./JG 27 and future Geschwader Kommodore Hptm. Neumann seen studying his map before crossing the Mediterranean.

I./JG 27 would quickly carve out a reputation in the desert. Without wishing to diminish the value of their pilots, the Germans' opponents were Hurricanes and Kittyhawks, aircraft inferior to the Bf 109. Favoring the defense of Britain, the RAF kept its precious Spitfires on home soil and it would be some 18 months before the first "Spit" was seen in African skies.

In the desert victories were quickly accumulated against an RAF more used to facing Italian biplanes. By late 1941, Marseille had gone from eight victories to 36; his rival Homuth had 33; Oblt. Ludwig Franzisket had twenty-seven. Oblt. Wolfgang Redlich, leading 1./JG 27, received the Knight's Cross on July 9 for his 21 victories. On December 5, when he was called to Luftwaffe HQ, he had 36. A slow scorer, Werner Schröer had been officially credited with just five *Abschüsse* in comparison. It should be noted that, despite the support of his Kommandeur, Marseille was still not well regarded by the hierarchy. Homuth and Franzisket both received the Knight's Cross for 22 victories (respectively on June 14 and July 23, 1941); Marseille, on the other hand, needed 50 before being awarded his.

But these claims had a price. During these months of combat, Marseille was forced to make three emergency landings and Schröer crash-landed twice (being wounded once). Although pilot losses in I./JG 27 were relatively few in number, some *Experten* were posted missing. On December 13, the promising Obfw. Albert Espenlaub (13 victories) was shot

Deployed to Africa on an emergency basis, many of JG 27's Bf 109s retained their European camouflage.

Marseille at the wheel of a Kubelwagen visiting the wreckage of one of the numerous P-40s that fell to his guns.

down by anti-aircraft fire near El Adem. Sent to a prison camp in Palestine, he was killed on February 25, 1942 attempting to escape.

Rommel's initiative led to a British counteroffensive, forcing the Luftwaffe to send II./JG 27 to Africa in September. The "star" of II./JG 27 was Ofw. Otto Schulz. He claimed three RAF fighters shot down on October 6 to open his scoring in North Africa. III./JG 27 followed in December. The ambitions of the "Desert Fox" thus forced the Luftwaffe to strip away fighter cover from an Eastern Front that already saw the Tagjäger thinly spread. The Bf 109 F of these two new Gruppen would also fight vigorously, but at that time, logistics proved difficult and shortages were frequent.

The new units also sustained losses. Lt. Gustav Langanke was posted missing as early as October 7, apparently shot down attacking a South African Maryland. He had not added to his score since claiming seven Tupolevs on June 25. Hptm. Wolfgang Lippert, leading II./JG 27, was shot down on 22 November over Bir el Gobi. With both legs broken, he died during the amputation in a Cairo hospital. Lippert was a Knight's Cross bearer and a five-victory Condor Legion ace who had been been credited with a further 25 victories. He had also downed five balloons. On December 24, Oblt. von Kageneck (9./JG 27) was shot down by a Hurricane. Seriously wounded, he died in hospital from blood poisoning.

If the German aces distinguished themselves in the Mediterranean theater, initially a very secondary arena, Rommel's desire for glory would require new aviation resources to be deployed to Africa. The German fighters may have come up against an opponent of inferior quality but the Allies had excellent rear bases in Egypt and, therefore, better logistics than the Axis. However, the Luftwaffe dominated the North African skies during 1941, thanks to the quality of its pilots but also to the excellent leadership of I./JG 27 by Edu Neumann.

Parade at I./JG 27 in the desert in front of a Bf 109 E.

In Profile:
Erbo Graf von Kageneck

Erbo Graf von Kageneck was born in Bonn on April 2, 1918, into nobility. A daredevil, like many young Germans stifled by Versailles he dreamed of flying. He thus entered the new Luftwaffe in 1936. At I./JG 1 in 1939, he champed at the bit but had to wait until the campaign in the West to claim his first four victories. After nine more successes over England, he was promoted to Kapitän of 9./JG 27 before making a name for himself over Malta in 1941. On July 30, 1941, after rapid success in the USSR, he was awarded the Knight's Cross for his 37 *Luftsiege*. After 65 victories he was awarded the Oak Leaves (October 26, 1941). When III./JG 27 was called to the Mediterranean, Erbo ran into his old RAF opponents and claimed two more fighters before being hit over Agedabia. He was able to land, although seriously injured. Transferred to hospital in Italy by boat, he died in Naples on February 12, 1942.

Like most high-scoring Luftwaffe aces, Kageneck was an excellent sports shot.

May 1941, Gela. Kapitän von Kageneck preparing to get airborne for Malta.

On the English Channel, 1941

Throughout early 1941, the RAF, well informed by Ultra, followed the transfers of Luftwaffe units to the East. By June 1941, there were only three fighter Geschwader operating on thc Western Front: JG 1, based mainly in the Netherlands; JG 26, deployed farther south and covering the sectors of Belgium and northern France; and JG 2, also spread farther south, protecting the rest of the French coast down as far as La Rochelle.

This weakness prompted British officials to launch what was dubbed the "Non-Stop Offensive," essentially an upsurge in daytime attacks from 17 June to late October 1941 targeting northern France and aimed at "writing down" the German fighters—principally of JG 2 and JG 26—using a handful of bombers as bait. Various tactics were employed, but all were basically large-scale fighter sweeps over a given sector, while the "Circus" was a joint operation with light bombers attacking factories or power plants. The means implemented were often disproportionate, with a handful of light or heavy bombers escorted by anything up to ten fighter squadrons. It was now the turn of the RAF to cross the Channel—the Battle of Britain in reverse. But in 1940, the main German goal had been political: to push Britain to surrender; in 1941, the RAF offensive was strategic. Most imagined that, within three months, the Wehrmacht would have finished off the Soviets. Then, as during the Great War, having drawn a line on the Eastern Front, the German army, boosted by its successes, could return in force to the West and, this time, a sea/land invasion was a real possibility.

During the late summer of 1941 the outstanding Luftwaffe fighter of the war, the Fw 190, was gradually introduced into service on the Channel coast

On the eve of *Barbarossa*, June 21, 1941—and indicating perhaps that the British, via Ultra, were aware of the imminent German invasion of the Soviet Union—the RAF mounted two successive circuses over northern France for the first time. Circus No. 16 targeted the airfield at Longuenesse (Saint-Omer) during the early afternoon—six Blenheims of 21 Sqn and an "escort" of no fewer than 15 squadrons of fighters. JG 26 alone intercepted, the German pilots claiming four victories. After scrambling from Audembert with his wingman Ofw. Bruno Hegenauer in tow, Kommodore Galland was soon up-sun and at altitude, launching a diving attack that pierced the RAF fighter screen to set one of the Blenheims alight. He claimed a second Blenheim shot down although this victory was not confirmed as his "victim" returned home. Galland's machine, an early-series Bf 109 F-2 (W.Nr. 5776) was hit by future ace Boleslaw "Ghandi" Drobinski of 303 Sqn—damage later assessed at 40 percent—but the Kommodore JG 26 was able to carry out a belly-landing close to the airfield at Calais-Marck before being picked up by a Bf 108 and ferried back to Audembert. Fw. Bruno Hagenauer bailed out near Saint-Omer while Gefr. Christian Knees of 9./JG 26 was shot down on his first sortie. II./JG 26 chasing after the RAF raiders also lost several machines to the Biggin Hill fighters, two pilots being shot down over the UK resulting in a largely positive outcome for the RAF from Circus No. 16: at least five JG 26 Bf 109s for one Blenheim and three fighters damaged.

Circus No. 17, mounted later that afternoon against the aerodrome at Desvres, resulted in II. Gruppe of the Richthofen being scrambled in support of the Schlageter over the coastal sector between Boulogne and Le Touquet to counter no fewer than 17 fighter squadrons escorting six 110 Sqn Blenheims. For the second time that day the fighting was largely favorable to the raiding RAF force. Kommodore Galland was airborne again, this time in his replacement Friedrich, minus a wingman. This was Bf 109 F-2 (W.Nr. 6713) (DG+MU) displaying a chevron and two bars.

Once again the Spitfires brought him down, although not before he claimed his 70th (probably the Spitfire of P.O. Edward of 616 Sqn which came down near Boulogne). Galland described the moments after being shot up as the most terrifying seconds of his life. Wounded in the head and the right arm, it was only with great difficulty that he managed to extricate himself from his doomed machine. W.Nr. 6713 crashed at Bellebrune, 12 kilometers east of

A yellow-nosed Friedrich of 8./JG 26 seen on the Channel coast during spring 1941.

Kommodore Galland, early 1941, with the Kommandeur I./JG 26, Hptm. Rolf Pingel.

Boulogne-sur-Mer. On landing Galland was taken to a farm by some "unpleasant looking Frenchmen" before being taken back to Audembert and on to the Kriegsmarine *Lazarett* (military hospital) at Hardinghem. Theo Osterkamp later drove over to inform Galland that his tally of victories (revised down to 69 as subsequently seen on the rudder scoreboard of his F-2 W.Nr. 6750) had now earned him the Knight's Cross of the Iron Cross with Oak Leaves and Swords (Ritterkreuz des Eisernen Kreuzes mit Eichenlaub und Schwertern). In addition to the Kommodore, JG 26 suffered three more losses.

II./JG 2 claimed no fewer than 11 victories (ten Spitfires and a single Hurricane), with the notable aces adding to their scores: Ofw. Kurt Bühligen (4./JG 2, three Spitfires), Lt. Siegfried Schnell (4./JG 2, two Spitfires west of Le Touquet), Oblt. Hans-Jürgen Hepe (4./JG 2, two Spitfires), and Kommandeur Greisert (a single Spitfire). These Spitfire claims were in addition to eight Spitfires claimed by JG 26. In total the RAF lost no more than four Spitfires against 19 German claims!

Seen here in June 1941, Oblt. Josef Priller's Bf 109 E-7 White 8 displays his personal emblem, an ace of hearts with the inscription "Jutta." The C3 fuel triangle above the *Kennziffer* (no. 8) is evidence of the installation of an up-rated DB 601 N engine.

In Profile:
Bf 109 "Emils"

Bf 109 Emil White 13 of 4./JG 77 with "black skeleton" emblem and eagle crest ahead of the cockpit as flown by the Staffelkapitän Helmut Henz during the Norwegian campaign, April 1940. Henz was a Condor Legion veteran who returned his first victory over an RAF Wellington twin-engine bomber on December 14, 1939. He shot down an RAF Blenheim twin-engine bomber near Stavanger on April 30, 1940. Promoted to Hauptmann and appointed Gruppenkommandeur of II./JG 77, Henz led the unit through the invasion of the Balkans but was shot down and killed off Crete on May 25, 1941.

Bf 109 Emil Yellow 2 (W.Nr. 5344), 3./JG 2, assigned to Helmut Wick and depicted as photographed following Wick's 18th victory on August 16, 1940. Appointed Staffelkapitän 3./JG 2 on June 22, 1940 Oblt. Wick was likely flying this machine on August 24 when he returned his 19th and 20th victories which "qualified" him for the award of the Knight's Cross. Within a matter of months, he would be appointed Kommodore—and shot down and killed south of the Isle of Wight. Just forward of the Staffel number is Wick's "hummingbird" emblem.

Bf 109 E White 13 (W.Nr. 1432), flown by Walter Oesau, Staffelkapitän 7./ JG 51 depicted as seen during the Battle of Britain. He was awarded the Knight's Cross on August 20, 1940, the fifth Jagdwaffe pilot to win the award.

Breakfast in late 1941 at Abbeville-Drucat. Knight's Cross bearers Wurmheller and Bühligen of JG 2 enjoy their coffee.

While generally described as Galland's worst day of the war—shot down twice—the Schlageter and the Richthofener were about to enjoy their most successful period of the conflict. Galland himself would be shot down again in another Friedrich on his next sortie on July 2—the leading Luftwaffe fighter ace downed three times in three consecutive sorties.

June 28 proved to a black day for JG 26. The modest Oblt. Gustav Sprick (leading 8./JG 26) was killed in combat with Spitfires near Holque, just north of Saint-Omer. With his score at 23 by the end of 1940, Sprick had returned his first kill of 1941 on June 16. In the space of eight days he then achieved seven further victories to progress his score to thirty-one. Early on June 28, all three Gruppen of JG 26 were airborne to intercept Circus No. 26, a raid on the power station at Comines. III./JG 26 was soon caught up in a dogfight with Spitfires of 303 Sqn. However, in attempting an evasive split-S maneuver at low altitude, Sprick apparently tore wings off his Bf 109 F-2 Black 4.

On July 23, 1941, two circuses were mounted for actual losses of 15 Spitfires and a single Hurricane shot down—the Richthofen claimed no fewer than 14 Spitfires during Circus No. 59 and more (plus a Hurricane) during Circus No. 60. JG 26 filed nine claims.

Two leading aces of the Stabsschwarm JG 2 seen during the late summer of 1941: Oblt. Erich Leie and Maj. Walter Oesau.

Operation *Sunrise*, July 24, 1941

July 24, 1941 was a significant day in the career of the Staffelführer 3./JG 2 Lt. Julius Meimberg:

> In the early afternoon the chief engineer (*Oberwerksmeister*) reported that my Bf 109 E-7 Yellow 1 was serviceable and suggested that I take it up for an air test. So I took off alone. Visibility was perfect. With the sun beating down on my canopy, temperatures rose rapidly in the cockpit and I climbed for altitude in search of cooler conditions.

Banking in the direction of Brest, Meimberg could clearly see the silhouette of the *Prinz Eugen* in the port. The *Gneisenau*, on the other hand, was lying in a huge dry dock. Meimberg then flew a wide curving turn to the northwest and caught sight of a series of black dots moving to the south at between 4,000 and 5,000 meters altitude.

> Bombers! They looked like swarms of insects; there was no doubt, however, they were bombers and there were several dozen of them. I struggled to remain calm. I quartered the sky looking for the escort. However, I saw no sign of condensation trails that might betray any fighters—not a single Spitfire. As the bombers were flying into the sun, it was likely that I had not yet been seen. I called up our command post and told them the number, the altitude and the heading of the intruders. The first enemy aircraft passed below me at that moment.

Meimberg feverishly switched on his sight and armed his MGs and dove down to come in behind a Handley-Page Hampden bomber.

> A long burst of fire ripped into his engines. He started to go down. I climbed back to altitude. After about ten minutes, I spotted another group of Hampdens and came down behind one of them. It wasn't long before he was joining my first victim. I again got back up-sun in an ambush position and, after a similar period, spotted my target: a Vickers Wellington. I came in from astern at full throttle and opened fire, exhausting the last of my ammunition. It went straight down and crashed, not giving any of its occupants a chance to escape. My third victory of the day! At that moment, the red low-fuel warning light started flashing on the instrument panel. I'd been airborne for more than an hour and it was high time to land. Suddenly, while still a long way from Guipavas, my engine coughed and sputtered and then stopped abruptly.

With his prop turned to fine pitch and still windmilling in the slipstream, the Staffelführer 3./JG 2 desperately sought out a landing strip before lining up on an open field in the vicinity of Brélès. In the ensuing forced landing Meimberg's Bf 109 came to a standstill after careening into a hedge and low wall. Severely damaged, the aircraft would be a write-off while the injured pilot did not return to his unit until spring 1942.

The first combat missions of a dangerous new adversary for the *Jagdflieger* were flown during the summer of 1941. Operation *Sunrise* was a daylight raid mounted on July 24, 1941 against the German battleships *Prinz Eugen*, *Scharnhorst,* and *Gneisenau* holed up in the port of Brest. The RAF committed their four-engine Halifax and Stirling bombers—and for the first time B-17 Flying Fortresses took part. The RAF's first B-17s were some 20 examples of the 38 B-17 Cs produced in the spring and early summer of 1941, designated Fortress I in RAF service and issued to 90 Sqn at Kinloss in Scotland. By 12 September 90 Sqn had carried out 22 raids, involving 39 Fortress sorties. Of those, 18 had been aborted, two had bombed secondary targets and 19 had bombed their primary targets. One of their least successful raids was the attempt to find and bomb the heavy cruiser *Admiral Scheer* anchored off Oslo on the morning of September 8, 1941. German fighters from I./JG 77 easily shot down two of the four Fortress Is dispatched. By September 1941 the British had lost, in combat and accidents, nearly half of their 20 B-17s. The performance of the Fortress confirmed the RAF in its belief that no daylight bomber could operate safely against the German air defenses.

The number of awards is evidence of the ferocity of combat over the Channel front during 1941 and the successes enjoyed by JG 2 and JG 26. On July 20, Oblt. Josef Priller (1./JG 26) obtained the Oak Leaves for 41 victories; on August 1, three Knight's Crosses were awarded to JG 2 pilots, Lt. Egon Mayer (21 victories), Oblt. Erich Leie (21 victories), and Oblt. Rudolf Pflanz (20 victories).

On August 12, Circus No. 69 targeting Saint-Omer and No. 70 Gosnay were again countered by JG 2's aces. Kommodore Maj. Walter Oesau was credited with no fewer than five Spitfires in 90 minutes, while Oblt. Erich Leie claimed three Spitfires. Hptm. Hans "Assi" Hahn (III./JG 2) added three more to his score and received the Oak Leaves on August 14 for his 42 victories. On September 4, Obfw. Josef Wurmheller (1./JG 2) received the Knight's Cross, not for 20 *Abschüsse* but for thirty-two.

September 20, 1941 was another bad day for the RAF with three circuses over France—JG 2 claimed 15 Spitfires (seven actual losses) while their training Staffel 4./JFS 5 claimed eleven. On September 27, two groups of 11 Blenheims were sent to Amiens and Mazingarbe (Circus No. 103). The RAF lost 12 Spitfires (from Nos 72, 129, 308, 403, 603, 609, 611, 615, and 616 Sqns).

Hahn was credited with his 50th victory following the circus flown on October 13 but he was still some way behind Lt. Siegfried Schnell, another JG 2 Oak Leaves recipient who had claimed his 50th during September. By the end of 1941, the Knight's Cross was being awarded more and more sparingly, even in the West.

But, as in all theaters of war, these victories came at a high price. On June 9, Oblt. Werner Machold, leading 7./JG 2, was shot down by anti-aircraft fire from a vessel off the coast of England before being captured. On July 3, the Kommodore of JG 2, Wilhelm Balthasar, was himself killed in combat near Saint-Omer. On July 10, another former Spain veteran, Hptm. Rolf Pingel, commanding I./JG 26, launched a reckless pursuit of an RAF bomber. Hit by the bomber's defensive fire, he was forced to put down near Dover and was captured.

In August, II./JG 26 left for a training course at Le Bourget to convert onto the new Fw 190 fighter type. The sleek BMW radial-engined design proved virtually vice-free after initial

Kommandeur III./JG 2 Hptm. Hans "Assi" Hahn, a great animal lover, alongside his rudder scoreboard with his Great Dane. Note the III. Gruppe band around the rear fuselage of his Friedrich.

On July 10, 1941, Bf 109 F-2 (W.Nr. 12764) was belly-landed along the Dover to Deal coast road near St. Margaret's Bay by Knight's Cross bearer and Kommandeur I./JG 26 Hptm. Rolf Pingel. Note the segmented spinner and the 22 victory markings on the rudder. Coded ES 906 by the RAF, the aircraft was extensively tested and eventually lost on October 20 1941.

teething problems were ironed out. Unlike the Bf 109, of which large numbers were lost in takeoff and landing accidents, it was of course a more modern design incorporating a basic engine management system to reduce the pilot's workload, electrically powered ancillary equipement and clear-vision canopy. It soon developed into a formidable machine and was appreciated by its pilots due to its combat qualities at low and medium altitudes. However, early difficulties, including engine fires, led to temporary restrictions: cross-Channel sorties, for example, were prohibited.

The first Fw 190 A-1 (W.Nr. 0028) went to the Kommandeur II./JG 26, Hptm. Walter Adolph. A former "Spaniard," on September 18 he clashed with Spitfires and was last seen diving toward the sea off Ostend. His body washed up on a beach on October 12. With 25 victories (one in Spain), he had been one of the first fighter pilots of the new Luftwaffe. On November 6, Hptm. Johann Schmid, leading 8./JG 26 and a Knight's Cross bearer since August 21, struck the waves north of Calais having just shot down his 45th victim.

The end of the year proved quieter, as the RAF licked its wounds. However, JG 26 lost its Kommodore on December 5. Following the disappearance of Mölders, the position of Inspector of Fighters was taken up by Galland, who left for Berlin. He soon became bogged down in the red tape inherent in any high command. JG 2 also lost its Kommodore when Walter Oesau (who had recently returned from the USSR

July 1941, the Fw 190 test center, Le Bourget, Paris. The commanding officer of this trials unit preparing the new fighter for service was the (later) Kapitän of 6./JG 26, Oblt. Otto Behrens. He is seen here (at left) with Galland, and Brown 6 in the background undergoing maintenance.

Göring visited JG 26 at Audembert on the Channel, December 5, 1941, to announce Galland's appointment as General der Jagdflieger. At the time, Galland had 95 kills in the West.

to command this Geschwader) reached 100 victories on 26 October, only the third Luftwaffe ace to achieve this after Werner Mölders and Günther Lützow. At 28 he had already been awarded the Swords for his 80th victory in July 1941. Like the late Mölders, he was banned from flying and passed through various commands. It would be two years before he was allowed to return to combat.

On December 22, 1941, JG 2 was shifted to Brest. With the depletion of fighter cover in the area of the Somme, the new Kommandeur of II./JG 26, J. Müncheberg, ordered 6./JG 26 to fly to Abbeville. His Kapitän, Oblt. Walter Schneider, a veteran with 20 victories, was reluctant to do so given the bad weather. But Müncheberg, who had recently returned from the Mediterranean, was insistent. He failed however to take account of the difficulties of flying over Western Europe in poor visibility. "Jap" Schneider took off with four pilots. All five hit the ground in the vicinity of Boulogne. Right up to his own disappearance, Müncheberg would maintain a feeling of guilt for having sent these five men to their deaths.

The "Non-Stop Offensive," although costly for the RAF, kept the German fighter arm on the alert on the English Channel. New aces appeared who, although struggling against a determined opponent, were able to win easier victories on the Continent than over England. To take an example from the two Geschwader fighting in France, Lt. Bruno Stolle (8./JG 2) achieved some ten victories at that time, and Lt. Paul Schauder (3./JG 26) a further nine. The Luftwaffe lost six talented Knight's Cross bearers in these commitments in the West but, despite this, the balance was still largely in favor of the Jagdgeschwader.

On October 26, 1941 the Kommodore of JG 2, Maj. Walter Oesau, returned his 100th victory and promptly received a *Flugverbot*. At 28 he had already been awarded the Swords for his 80th victory in July 1941. Although officially banned from flying, he continued to fly combat for several weeks thereafter.

Lt. Paul Schauder (3./JG 26) checks the application of a victory bar on the rudder of his 109. He survived the war, credited with 21 victories.

Kommandeur I./JG 26 Hptm. Johannes Seifert (right) observes Fw 190 A-2 White 4 running up. The Fw 190 was still subject to certain teething problems, such as engine fires.

Fw 190 A-1 Brown 13 of 6./JG 26. The first Fw 190s arrived at II./JG 26 during the summer of 1941, the first Jagdgruppe to receive the new type.

February 1942, Briansk. 4./JG 51 Bf 109 F White 12 about to get airborne for a sortie, photographed in front of a hangar.

Over the USSR, 1942

In 1942, the Eastern theater of operations was critical. If the Wehrmacht could dominate the Red Army, it could return en masse to the West and finally force the decision there. From the aerial viewpoint, the Eastern Front featured two key sticking points during the first part of 1942. Firstly, the northern sector: the belligerents were locked in battle for Leningrad, hence the long siege maintained in part by JG 54, that resulted in a devastating famine. Secondly, the southern sector: the fortress of Sevastopol was the focus in this sector of the front.

After the bloodletting of *Barbarossa*, "Red" air power was growing stronger. The separate peace with Japan—the Soviet-Japanese Neutrality Pact of April 1941—had allowed Moscow to transfer air units from Asia westward. But, above all, aviation factories were withdrawn to the Urals, far beyond the range of German bombers. This colossal move made it possible to produce older aircraft while initiating the construction of more modern fighters. From April 1942, Luftwaffe claims increasingly mentioned more Yak and MiG fighters.

The list of German fighter units engaged in the East during 1942 is surprisingly short: JG 3, JG 5,

A Staffel (JG 51) still equipped with Bf 109 E in the harsh Russian winter of 1941/42, at Stolzy.

Aces of JG 51, Schack, Thiel, and Jennewein at Orel, February 23, 1942. Lt. Günther Schack returned his first victory in 7./JG 51 on July 23, 1941 but did not become an ace until July 30, 1942. By the end of 1942 he had some 23 victories, having claimed five Pe-2s on December 17 in the Velikiye Luki area. He was awarded the Knight's Cross on October 29, 1943 for 117 victories, and commanded I./JG 51.

JG 51, JG 52, JG 54, and JG 77, all told some 500 aircraft to cover a front from Finland to the Black Sea. Not surprisingly, in comparative terms the successes of the day fighter aces started to diminish. JG 53, withdrawn from the Eastern Front, deployed to the Mediterranean. During the first quarter of 1942, II./JG 3 also fought temporarily in Malta while I./JG 3, rested in the Netherlands, and did not return until May. The remaining German fighter units were scattered. JG 51, re-equipping with the Fw 190, shifted from sector to sector and from front to front. I. and II./JG 52 were withdrawn from the Eastern Front at the beginning of the year for rest and refit.

In the far north, JG 5 fought alongside the Finnish Air Force, harassing Murmansk and the Arctic sea routes to the USSR. The fighting was very fierce in this area where the Eismeergeschwader, the Arctic squadrons, faced elite Soviet units. Particularly talented pilots such as Obfw. Rudolf Müller, Lt. Heinrich Ehrler, and Lt. Theodor Weissenberger stood out. All would receive the Knight's Cross that year.

On January 1, 1942 the Stab. and III. Gruppe JG 77 were at Sarabus in the Crimea and would spend the first four months of the year both in this sector and on the Kertsch peninsula. II./JG 77 had been sent "home" to Vienna for rest and refit and would not return to

Aces of I./JG 51. From left: Heinrich Krafft (awarded the Knight's Cross on March 18, 1942), Oblt. Heinz Bär, Lt. Erwin Fleig (hidden behind Bär), and Lt. Heinrich Höfemeier (awarded the Knight's Cross on April 5, 1942).

Hptm. Heinz Bär (right) replaced Ihlefeld as Kommandeur I./JG 77 in May 1942 and passed 100 victories on 19 May. Both are seen here, possibly commenting on Bär's rudder scoreboard.

the front until March 1942. A new I./Gruppe was established with the renaming of Hptm. Herbert Ihlefeld's I.(J)/LG 2 which had operated in close conjunction with the Stab/JG 77 since the invasion. The Gruppe was now incorporated permanently into JG 77. Aside from the Kommandeur, who had returned 50 victories and been awarded the Knight's Cross, the Gruppe had other experienced pilots on its roster such as Oblt. E. Erwin Clausen and Günther Hannak, Lt. E. Friedrich Geisshardt, and Heinz-Edgar Berres, all of whom would be awarded the Knight's Cross over the course of the following months. This new I. Gruppe soon moved to Stalino and Kharkov, while 1. Staffel deployed to Romania and in late April formed the unit tasked with protecting the Ploesti oilfields before being renamed 1./JG 4 in late July.

On February 16, the talented Hptm. Heinz Bär (12./JG 51) received the Swords for his 90 *Abschüsse*. Hans Philipp, leading I./JG 54, received them on March 12 after 86 victories. Bär replaced Ihlefeld as Kommandeur I./JG 77 in early May and passed 100 victories on 19 May, downing five Ratas over the Kertsch peninsula for his victories 99–103. The following day's OKW *Bericht* (report): "Hptm. Baer, Gruppenkommandeur in einem Jagdgeschwader yesterday achieved his victories 99–103 … Das Jagdgeschwader 77 has now raised its victory total to 2,011."

During June 1942, Hptm. Herbert Ihlefeld was appointed Kommodore of JG 52. He was injured in combat on July 22 1942 and after his convalescence, appointed to command training school Jagdfliegerschule 3.

Oblt. Heinrich Setz learns of the death of a comrade.

II./JG 77 returned to the front on March 17, 1942 and scored heavily two days later as Oblt. Heinrich Setz, Staka 4./JG 77 recalled:

> We knocked down 21 "Ruskis" and I got five of them for my 50th victory. I was airborne for the first sortie of the day at 08:00. Eight of the most modern bombers [Pe-2s] with a strong escort appeared overhead at about the same time. In matter of seconds the infantry fighting below us received a present from me—my 46th and 47th victories. During this time my wingman—Uffz. Ernst-Wilhelm Reinert—shot down his 29th. The impact of the new cannon was impressive. I can still recall some of the difficulties we used to encounter when shooting down Russian bombers. Now they are literally blown apart.

Setz is referring here to the new F-4 toting an engine-mounted MG 151/20 with which his Gruppe had re-equipped. By April 30, II. Gruppe had claimed 104 enemy aircraft destroyed for the loss of six killed or missing; the leading ace of the Gruppe was Setz with 61 and the next highest scorer was Ofw. Rudolf Schmidt with forty-two. Schmidt however had been killed in his Bf 109 F-4 Black 15 on April 6, shot down over the Crimea in combat with Pe-2 bombers.

III./JG 77 was withdrawn from the front on March 20, having filed 90 claims for the loss of one pilot since January 1, 1942. Kommandeur Ubben was the leading ace with 70

On April 10, 1942 the Kommandeur of IV./JG 51, Maj. Karl-Gottfried Nordmann (left), was appointed Geschwader Kommodore. He had returned some 70 kills and been awarded the Oak Leaves. He was injured on June 26 after ground-looping his Bf 109 Friedrich W.Nr. 12825 and did not return to the unit until October. His temporary replacement was Maj. Müncheberg. In the short time he was with the Gechwader during 1942, Müncheberg returned 33 victories, including his 100th on September 5, 1942.

victories followed by Emil Omert who had 45 and had been awarded the Knight's Cross on 19 March for 40 victories. Ubben and Huy received the Oak Leaves on March 12 and May 17 respectively, the first JG 77 pilots to do so. Ihlefeld was awarded the Swords for this 100th on April 22.

The new Kommodore of JG 77, Hptm. Gordon M. Gollob, had arrived in mid-May from a period as a shadow Kommodore with JG 54 after serving as Kommandeur II./JG 3 and having spent several months at the Erprobungsstelle Rechlin (test center). He was credited with 86 victories and had received the Oak Leaves. His organizational skills were put to good use since, at that time, he was responsible for coordinating all Luftwaffe fighter units in the area. The May 14 entry in his diary reads:

> I flew with Handrick from airfields close to the front. In the Kertsch breakthrough area things look great! The sweet smell of corpses pollutes the air up to us in the Storch. On the 1st day of the attack there were about 2,000 aircraft over the Russians! A picture of infernal destruction and bitter resistance … After I have studied the enemy situation, which ultimately determines how our aircraft should be deployed, we can get started.

On May 16th Hptm. Gollob shot down his first enemy over the Kertsch front and by May 20 this number had increased to 14, for Gollob's 100th. On June 2, 1942, the Axis opened Operation *Störfang* (*Sturgeon Catch*), the onslaught against the besieged Soviet forces in the Crimean port of Sevastopol. Gollob's diary entry for June 3 reads:

> The successes of our fighters outweigh our losses. Dogfighting near the ground brings avoidable losses due to the enormous small arms and anti-aircraft fire. I forbade them at first. The pilot situation is bad, partly due to losses in air combat and injuries, but also by detachments from the mission. Not everyone is up to the enormous physical and nervous strain. It is more sensible—and more humane—to replace unstable pilots in time before they infect others and fall themselves.

Gollob returned his 102nd victory, another LaGG-3 on June 7:

> Today our fighters returned 9 victories. An officer and a non-commissioned officer are missing. The Russian flies desperately and quite well. My 102nd kill, a LaGG-3, went down in flames on the airfield of Sevastopol VI. But I had a lucky escape myself. With the radiator shot through, I barely reached my own lines. My mechanics painted an oak wreath with the number 100 on my rudder. The "black men" should really have their own award, because what these soldiers accomplish—in untiring, exact, and conscientious work—cannot be put into words.

The new Kommodore of JG 77, Hptm. Gordon M. Gollob.

In Profile:
Bf 109 "Emil" and "Friedrichs"

Bf 109 E-7 White 8 flown by the Staffelkapitän of 1./JG 26 Josef Priller. Priller had claimed his 20th victory on October 17, 1940 and was awarded the Knight's Cross. This was his last victory with JG 51. On November 19 he was appointed Staffelkapitän 1./JG 26. It was not until June 16, 1941 that he returned his 21st. Note his personal ace of hearts playing card emblem.

Bf-109 F-4 / R1 (W.Nr. 13249) Black 2, Lt. Wolfram Stecher, 8./JG 77. Emil Omert noted in his diary for May 13, 1942; "*Unternehmen Fredericus* [Operation *Fredericus*, launch of the 1942 summer offensive at Kharkov and the start of *Fall Blau*, the drive to Stalingrad]. Lt. Wolfram Stecher from my Staffel shot down and killed."

A Bf 109 Friedrich of JG 54, the "green heart" Geschwader. Note the improved aerodynamic profile of this variant: rounded wingtips, spinner, absence of stabilizer struts and retractable tailwheel.

On June 21:

> The haze and smoke over Sevastopol makes any horizontal visibility impossible. So far I have reported 103 *Abschüsse*, but I have yet to file four more victory claims, in order not to reach the "100" too quickly. Almost certainly an *Einsatzverbot* [ban on flying sorties] is likely. Today I in fact returned my 107th *Abschuss*.

On June 23, 1942, Gollob was awarded the Swords to his Knight's Cross. The fortress of Sevastopol finally capitulated in early July after weeks of intense bombardment.

With the Crimea conquered, Hitler launched his famous *Fall Blau* (Case Blue), the 1942 summer strategic offensive in southern Russia. Marshal Fedor von Bock's army was to seize Isjum. The main offensive would thus open the way to Voronezh on the Don, then to Stalingrad where the troops could set up their winter quarters. The Caucasus would be conquered in the process, which would then allow the Germans to focus on Leningrad. This ambitious plan met with some opposition.

According to some, Hitler had no choice but to push toward the Caucasus oilfields: he needed fuel. However, Stalin did too. The Red Army was therefore going to have to resist rather than retreat. The USSR had already lost Krivoi Rog's steel production and Nicopol's manganese. The quality of Soviet armor was beginning to suffer, but if *Blau* succeeded, Stalin would have no coal or oil left. *Blau* was launched on June 28, 1942 with some initial success. The German and Hungarian divisions led by General Maximilian von Weichs broke the Soviet front and pushed towards Voronezh. Two days later, the 6th Army began its advance toward the Don. The first signs of a looming disaster began to emerge: fuel supplies were only available until mid-September. And the results of the first battles were disappointing in terms of prisoners and spoils of war—a sign that the Soviets had learned their lesson: they would never again be surrounded. Hitler had anticipated an elastic defense but relied on the speed of his panzers to prevent the retreat of the enemy to the other side of the Don.

In the air "Stalin's Falcons" had also learned the lessons of 1941 and favored formation flights, having abandoned the suicide attacks of *Barbarossa*'s early days. The Tagjäger in the East thus continued to record victories, but at a much reduced pace. The easier victories of 1941 had dried up. The figures were more modest with peaks during highly contested engagements in strategic locations. The Bf 109 was still feared and remained a formidable opponent alongside the Fw 190. A new danger emerged in a critical sector for the Tagjagd. During the night of June 11/12, 1942, 13 American B-24s were airborne from Africa to bomb Romanian oil installations. This operation, known as *Halpro*, an apparently unsuccessful test, was in fact a real threat. The Luftwaffe subsequently decided to strengthen the defense of the sector.

The numerical inferiority of the Luftwaffe, the increasing quality of the Soviet pilot, and similar considerations should not indicate that the position of the Tagjäger had become untenable in the East. The number of Knight's Crosses awarded that year would even seem to prove the opposite; by this stage, the fighter ace required at least 50 victories to win the award. The lightning career of Oblt. Hermann Graf, Staka of 9./JG 52, demonstrates this. The latter received the Knight's Cross on January 24, 1942 for his 45 victories, all won in the East; on May 17, i.e. four months later, Graf was awarded the Oak Leaves (105 victories) and, two days later, the Swords.

In mid-August, III./JG 52 had moved forward to provide air cover as the army tried to establish bridgeheads across the Kuban River. Kommodore Gollob was temporarily appointed to command JG 52 after Maj. Herbert Ihlefeld was severely injured in a takeoff accident. On August 14, Gollob and Graf were the two highest-scoring pilots in the East, both having achieved 120 victories. Graf was then reassigned to lead a detachment of experienced aces from III./JG 52 to cover the assault on Stalingrad under the command of JG 3's Hptm. Wolf-Dietrich Wilcke.

Initially Graf was based at Tuzov and then Pitomnik west of the city. Stalingrad was critical to both sides. It was strongly defended and became the focus of intense air battles. Graf and his colleagues no longer faced obsolescent aircraft, as they had in the south. Flying four or five sorties a day, Graf invariably ended the day with two or three victories. During August Graf filed 29 claims bringing his tally to 140 kills. On September 16, 1942, he received the Diamonds for 172 victories, the fifth member of the Wehrmacht to receive the award and the top-scoring ace in the Luftwaffe. Within the space of eight months, he had received all four levels of the Knight's Cross and was soon promoted to Hauptmann. On September 17, he claimed three more victories—two LaGGs and an IL-2—but a 20-mm Soviet cannon shell went through his canopy, narrowly missing his head. On September 20, he bagged another LaGG but returned to Pitomnik with a misfiring engine and a shot-up radiator, gliding across the Volga in a shallow descent. Three days later he downed ten Soviet machines, recording the exploit in his diary:

> Yesterday, September 23, was my most successful day ever. Dawn was only just breaking as we got airborne. At 3,000 meters Heinrich Füllgrabe and I crossed no-man's land, some 100 kilometers behind the front. The sun was rising over Stalingrad. The city was shrouded in huge clouds of smoke from the many fires still ablaze there. Suddenly we caught sight of two fast Russian bombers ahead of us. We quickly moved in behind them and opened up with our first bursts of fire. Five fighters were providing top cover for them. In barely twenty seconds three of them were tumbling earthwards. We were briefly caught up in a turning fight with the others, but I managed to break off and set off after the bombers. One of the Russian fighters gave chase but couldn't make up the distance. Up above Heinrich

At the end of April 1942, the Führer presented decorations to pilots fighting in the East. From left: Hptm. Herbert Ihlefeld leading I./LG 2 (Swords for 132 kills), Wolf-Dieter Huy leading 7./JG 77 (Oak Leaves for 32 victories, his arm in a sling after taking a bullet), and Wolfgang Späte leading 5./JG 54 (Oak Leaves for 79 kills). The ceremony had been delayed due to Huy's injury. Unusually, these three aces all survived the war.

> had his hands full. The rear gunner gave me a well-aimed salvo as I closed in but this machine too was soon plunging earthwards. We broke off and headed home with six victories, four of them mine. In the afternoon—my fourth sortie—I downed my fifth and sixth and at 14:30 and 14:31 I accounted for my seventh and eighth, all of them bombers. In the early evening I flew a sortie in my lightly armed Yellow 3—two cannon and two MGs. At 16:38 and 16:55 two more enemy machines fell to my guns for a total of ten victories.

On September 25 Graf's tally stood at 199. No fighter ace had achieved 200 victories. Graf recalled the morning sortie flown on September 26, 1942 during which he became the first pilot in aviation history to claim 200 enemy aircraft shot down:

> we scrambled on another sortie. Almost immediately my wingman reported an engine malfunction and had to abort. As I carried on alone I was not too keen to perform any "heroics." I spotted a group of MiGs circling in the vicinity of our field. As they sighted me, one of them broke formation and headed down towards me, presumably their commander looking for what he thought might be an easy kill over a lone Bf 109. At long range he snapped out a burst. His aim was good. I hunched behind the armor plate of my G-2 as his tracers went whizzing past the cockpit, rattling against the wings and fuselage. I threw the stick forward and put the nose down to pick up speed and then pulled up hard. The MiG pilot was not expecting such a maneuver—he seemed to hesitate for a moment. Outdistancing him in the climb, I rolled my crate over on one wing and swooped down on the MiG still climbing after me. A long burst tore into his fuselage. The enemy machine began to belch flame and spun down, soon slamming into the ground. As I departed the scene, the other MiGs made no attempt to follow, probably shaken by the death of their comrade. I touched down at the western end of the airfield at Pitomnik. This was my 200th victory.

The 62 victories claimed by Graf in that single month (of September) remain a record unbeaten in aviation history. Elevated to hero status by the Luftwaffe, he was promoted to Major on September 29, and issued a *Flugverbot*. The whole of JG 52 gathered at Soldatskaja to congratulate him before he flew back to Berlin a few days later.

No fewer than 28 Oak Leaves were distributed in the East in 1942. Following his 81st victory on 23 June, Heinrich Setz received the award which was presented at the Führerhauptquartier (Führer Headquarters) at Rastenburg on 28/29 June. Two other Luftwaffe officers were presented with the Oak Leaves that day by Hitler, the night-fighter

Bf 109 F-4 Black 5 flown by the Kapitän of 5. Staffel JG 77, Oblt. "Toni" Hackl. He achieved his 100th *Abschuss* during August 1942.

Walter Nowotny of 3./JG 54 with his *erster Wart* (lead mechanic) seen in the spring of 1942.

pilot Hptm. Helmut Lent and fellow JG 77 pilot Oblt. Friedrich Geisshardt. Following their return to the front, JG 77 was assigned to the newly created Army Group B in support of *Fall Blau*. Setz claimed two MiG-3s on July 23 and the next day, July 24, he reached his 100th. He was the 13th Luftwaffe pilot to achieve the century mark. Barely a week later on August 3, the Kapitän of 5. Staffel JG 77, Oblt. "Toni" Hackl, achieved his 100th *Abschuss* and the Oak Leaves followed after 106 victories (109th award of the Oak Leaves).

These were impressive figures but, henceforth, this decoration would be awarded for an average of 140 victories. But there were also a significant number of decorations awarded posthumously during 1942 in the East: on March 12, Hptm. Franz Eckerle, Kommandeur I./JG 54, was forced to abandon his Bf 109 hit by anti-aircraft fire near Velikije Luki, after winning his 59th victory, but was immediately shot by Soviet soldiers. A member of the Luftwaffe since 1936, he led 6./JG 54 and won four victories in the West (over England, he had operated mainly in the *Jabo* role).

Between June and November 1942, some 20 German fighter aces each with 40 or more individual victories were lost on the Eastern Front. The following are some of the most notable: on 23 June, the young Austrian pilot Leopold Steinbatz was shot down by anti-aircraft fire in a wood near Woltschanck. He had joined 9./JG 52 at the end of 1940 and flew as Graf's wingman. Promoted to Leutnant posthumously he was the only non-commissioned officer to be awarded the Swords, being credited with 99 *Abschüsse*. The Sudeten Lt. Edgard Hübner (posted during the spring of 1941 to III./JG 3) had a meteoric career. On March 28, 1942, after winning his 47th victory, an IL-2 near Staraja Russa, he disappeared and was posthumously awarded the Knight's Cross.

On May 22, Lt. Hans Strelow (Kapitän of 5./JG 51) was shot down near Mszensk by the machine-gunner of a DB-3, his last victim. Strelow had been awarded the Knight's Cross on March 18. He was credited with seven more kills

Silverskaja, 1942. Hans-Ekkehard Bob (9./JG 54), with back to the camera, has organized a celebration for Obfw. Wilhelm Schilling, on the occasion of his 500th *Feindflug*. Schilling, wounded shortly afterwards, received the Knight's Cross for his 48 victories, was an instructor for a while and then returned to command 9./JG 54. He would fight until the end of the war, achieving 63 victories. Lt. Eugen-Ludwig Zweigart is on the right.

On May 22, after being forced down behind Soviet lines, Lt. Hans Strelow shot himself rather than be taken captive by Russian troops. This 5./JG 51 Oak Leaves bearer was 20 years old.

Long-serving Staffelkapitän of 9./JG 3 Oblt. Viktor Bauer shot down four enemy machines on July 25 to take his total past 100 for which he was awarded the Oak Leaves the following day. He was taken off ops after another four victories achieved on August 9.

the same day and a further three the following day. He had been awarded the Oak Leaves on March 24 for 66 victories and received the award from Hitler on his 20th birthday at the Führerhauptquartier two days later. After a lengthy spell of home leave, he resumed combat with his Staffel on May 22 in Briansk. Airborne with his wingman Uffz. Bergmann in Bf 109 F Black 10 (W.Nr. 8239), Strelow flew a free hunt over Orel. The pair came across a lone DB-3 which Bergmann disabled before Strelow closed in for the *Fangschuss*, or coup de grâce. A burst of fire from the rear gunner shredded Strelow's rudder and forced him down behind Russian lines. A rescue sortie—*Rettungseinsatz*—was attempted but on returning to Strelow's force-landed Friedrich, the machine was seen to be surrounded by Russian troops. Strelow had always maintained that he would never allow himself to enter Russian captivity. It was assumed that on seeing *Rotarmisten*—Red troops—approaching, Strelow had committed suicide. He was never heard of again.

On August 2, 1942, Hptm. Richard Leppla, Kommandeur III./JG 51, suffered a serious eye injury in combat. He attempted to remain at the front and continue combat flying but was seriously injured when, five days later, he struck a landing Ju 52 on takeoff from Juchnow in his Bf 109 F-2 (W.Nr. 8185). In December he was posted as Kommandeur of training school JFS 5. In April 1945, he was appointed to head JG 6 and finished the war with 68 victories.

On July 22, Kommandeur III./JG 3 Maj. Karl-Heinz Greisert was killed. Greisert had enjoyed a successful career in the West with JG 2 and had returned 33 victories. On August 10, Staffelkapitän of 9./JG 3, Oblt. Viktor Bauer, was injured in the crash-landing of his Bf 109 F-4 (W.Nr. 13241) at Nowo-Kalatsch and never returned to the front. Three more aces disappeared on the same day, August 10: Carl Sattig, 56 victories, Staffelkapitän of 6./JG 54, was downed and captured near Rzhev; Lt. Helmut Macher of 2./JG 53, was taken captive after his Bf 109 G-2 Black 11 (W.Nr. 13431) was hit by ground fire southwest of Stalingrad; Obfw. Heinrich Leschert of 3./JG 53 was reported missing in Bf 109 G-2 Yellow 1 (W.Nr. 13430), crashing after being hit by debris from a Russian machine in combat in the Stalingrad area.

On August 13, Lt. Ernst Weismann had to bail out near Rzhev in enemy territory. Born in Austria, he had been posted to a front unit in March 1941. In 12./JG 51, he downed 69 Soviet aircraft but, while his wingman saw him landing on August 13, he subsequently went missing. He was awarded the Knight's Cross and the rank of Oberleutnant, posthumously, having been presumed killed by the enemy. Another Sudeten, Lt. Waldemar Semelka, had been posted in fall 1941 to 4./JG 52. The German offensive of 1942 allowed him to win several victories—including 21 in one week. On August 21, 1942, he shot down two Boston bombers (74th and 75th victories) near Sdrenala-Achtuiba and was reported missing. The Knight's Cross was awarded posthumously.

Fw. Franz Schulte, one of the aces of 6. Staffel JG 77 with 46 victories, made a successful belly-landing in enemy territory north of Priwalowka during the fighting for Voronezh on August 12 and was reported missing. The Knight's Cross was awarded to him on September 24—albeit posthumously since he was never heard of again. A further two 6. Staffel pilots were also forced to bail out on August 12. One of them was able to return to German lines but the second, Uffz. Hans Höger, was captured:

> On my last combat encounter, Lt. Badum led the Staffel in the air because our Staffelkapitän, Oblt. Clausen, was at Hitler's Rastenburg headquarters to receive the Oak Leaves. My 109 took hits in the engine from a Russian aircraft that came out of the sun. The Bf 109 caught fire immediately and I jettisoned the canopy to jump. The slipstream kept me firmly pinned to the back of the seat and the rear of the cockpit, but after a struggle, I managed to free myself and let myself go. For a terrible moment I remained hooked up on the antenna mast, which damaged the parachute. Again I had to fight to get free. When the parachute finally deployed barely one hundred meters from the ground, the shock was such that my boots were torn off. I landed safe and sound, and in my bare feet set off in the direction of our lines on a

Although not quite as fast as the Bf 109 G-2, JG 51's new Fw 190s were much sturdier and with four cannon and two machine guns were powerfully armed, ideal for taking on the heavily armored IL-2 Sturmoviks.

> long trek. I hid by day and heading in a southerly direction, got my bearings at night from the stars and my arm compass. I had nothing to eat and drink, but for the morning dew and some cereals picked in the fields. I passed numerous Russian convoys. Suddenly on the evening of the third day, 15 August, a voice called out, "*Stoï!*" A Soviet patrol had spotted me. Captivity and all its sufferings began at that moment and would last six long years.

Many of the German aces lost in this way were "go-getters": the quest for kills and medals seems to have overridden all other considerations: filing a claim for an enemy aircraft at all costs even skewed fighting efficiency. Their disappearance during this period suggests that the air situation in the East in 1942 was no longer quite the same as it had been in 1941. But, despite this, the *Luftsiege* on the Eastern Front continued to devalue. On September 4, 1942, the future ace Walter Nowotny, of 3./JG 54, was awarded his Knight's Cross having achieved 56 victories!

During September 1942 no fewer than five aces of JG 3 were awarded the Knight's Cross for reaching 50 victories, including Ofw. Otto Wessling, Oblt. Helmut Mertens, and Lt. Wilhelm Lemke. Lemke had been appointed Kapitän of 9./JG 3 following the disappearance of 29-victory ace Lt. Rolf Diergardt just days after this latter ace had replaced Kapitän Bauer at the head of 9. Staffel on August 10, 1942. JG 3 was operating in the south, covering the drive toward Stalingrad having been transferred from the Demyansk Pocket. III./JG 3 lost seven aces during this period, May–September 1942.

But, for determined pilots, the Eastern Front still allowed some high scores. I./JG 53 had been transferred urgently to the East and its pilots quickly carved out reputations. On September 23, 1942, Fw. Walter Crinius (3./JG 53) received the Knight's Cross and the Oak Leaves simultaneously for his 100 victories. He had astonishingly been able to accumulate this scorecard in just three months, his first victory having been obtained on June 9, 1942. He would then be promoted to officer. The next day, Oblt. Wolfgang Tonne, his comrade and rival, would also receive the Oak Leaves for his 101 victories. He had claimed 88 Soviet aircraft downed in only 156 sorties. Neither of these two *Experten* experienced difficulty in "changing fronts."

Late in August 1942, Hptm. Heinrich Krafft's I./JG 51 became the first fighter unit to re-equip with the Fw 190 on the Eastern Front having converted onto the Fw 190 A-3 at Jesau near Königsberg. The robust new fighter was superior in most respects to the Bf 109: weight of fire, engine reliability in cold weather and its relative invulnerability to combat damage. Oblt. Erich Leie, who

At right is Kommandeur I./JG 51, Hptm. Heinrich Krafft, 78-victory ace, killed in action, December 14, 1942.

Oblt. Georg Schentke standing on the wing of his 9./JG 3 Friedrich Yellow 8, May 1942. Schentke was one of the most successful aces of the Platzschutzstaffel (Airfield Defense Squadron) Pitomnik, a small ad-hoc unit that flew sorties from the airfield within the city of Stalingrad. He was shot down over Stalingrad on Christmas Day 1942 and subsequently listed as missing. Some sources credit him with as many as 90 victories.

had fought over Dieppe in France the previous month, was posted from I./JG 2 to I./JG 51 in order to help the "Mölders" pilots on the new type. Flying one of his first sorties in the East on September 10 as Krafft's wingman, the two aces ran into four IL-2s; Leie downed two in four minutes, thus scoring the first Eastern Front victories in a Focke-Wulf 190.

During this period I./JG 51 primarily flew operations in defense of the Demyansk Pocket, covering supply transports. The first victory at the new front was returned on October 23 by Hptm. Krafft, who shot down a LaGG-3 east of Lagodnaya Divina. Krafft scored at regular intervals: on November 26, the Germans intercepted a group of eight low-flying IL-2s, Krafft downing three, whereas one machine fell to his wingman, Hptm. Riemann. Four days later "Gaudi" Krafft shot down another Sturmovik for his 70th victory and on December 4 claimed five. On December 10, Riemann was killed in a clash with LaGG-3s north of Sichevka. Hptm. Krafft downed an LaGG and a Pe-2 bomber. However, on December 14, Krafft's luck ran out too, when his Fw 190 A-3 (W.Nr. 130539) Black << was downed by Soviet flak south of Belyi. Krafft apparently survived the bailout but was killed on the ground.

During December, the first group of I./JG 54 pilots picked up their new Fw 190s at Heiligenbeil in East Prussia, led by Hptm. Hans Philipp. The Gruppe was involved in the defense of the Demyansk Pocket, fighting off ever-stronger Soviet air attacks. On December 16, Philipp downed three MiG-3s and one Yak-4 and on the December 30 no fewer than five LaGG-3s and three Sturmoviks, thus reaching 128 victories.

At the end of 1942, the *Schwerpunkt*, the main concentration of effort on the Eastern Front, was Stalingrad. The Wehrmacht entered the city but, after initial successes, encountered strong resistance from the Red Army. The 6th Army was surrounded on November 23.

Ofw. Eberhard von Boremski's 9./JG 3 Bf 109 F-4 Yellow 4 (W.Nr. 13220) displaying the 43 victory bars that earned him the Knight's Cross in May 1942. His final total was 104. He survived the war and Soviet captivity.

Lt. Franz-Josef Beerenbrock (born 1920) was one of those aces with a list of achievements entirely accumulated in the East. Arriving in March 1941 at 10./JG 51, he was captured near Welish on November 9, 1942 and returned from captivity seven years later. He had 117 Soviet aircraft to his credit and wore the Oak Leaves.

Wrongly, Feldmarschall Göring and his entourage believed they could repeat the "miracle" of the Demjansk airlift. The *Kessel* (cauldron) airfields in Stalingrad were heavily defended, especially the Luftwaffe airfield at Pitomnik.

The German pilots—in particular of JG 3 Udet—struggled in vain. Oblt. Georg Schentke of 2./JG 3 flew into Pitomnik in December 1942 and on the 12th shot down six aircraft (78–83 victories) while Kommodore Maj. Wolf-Dietrich Wilcke returned his victories 145–148 and passed 150 on December 17, downing three Yaks. Schentke shot down his 86th victim on Christmas Day, but was hit himself and had to parachute into enemy lines. Having started his career in March 1940, taken part in the campaign in the West and been awarded the Knight's Cross in September 1941, Schentke was reported missing. For his part, Maj. Wolf-Dietrich Wilcke was awarded the Swords on December 23 for his 156 victories. But individual achievements could hardly impact the course of events, even if JG 3 had reported some 200 Soviet machines shot down over the besieged city.

While the Stalingrad Pocket dominated the end of 1942, the Germans were still in trouble over the central northern sector of the front where the Demyansk siege, the focus of constant fighting during 1942, was still ongoing and where two Soviet fronts had surrounded the town of Velikije Luki. Large formations of IL-2s harassed German positions defended by II. and III./JG 54. On November 29, Ofw. Max Stotz scored his 100th and on December 30 returned ten kills, bringing his score to 129.

Fw 190 JG 51, Wjasma, during the winter of 1942/3. Having managed just 18 victories in over 450 combat sorties with the Bf 109, Lt. Günther Schack added 22 victories to his tally in his first 40 combat flights with the Fw 190 from mid-December 1942.

In the West, 1942

The end of the Non-Stop Offensive and the winter had slowed air activity on the Channel. The Kriegsmarine took advantage to spring the battleships *Scharnhorst* and *Gneisenau*—holed up in Brest since March 1941—from the trap in which they found themselves. They had become one of Bomber Command's priority targets. Operation *Donnerkeil*—the so-called "Channel Dash"—was launched to take place in very bad weather to hinder the RAF and coastal artillery.

On the evening of February 11, 1942, the two ships, with a maritime escort, set sail. To ensure air coverage, some 90 Bf 109s and Fw 190s of JG 2, a further 90 JG 26 fighters and 60 aircraft of JG 1 flew over the convoy from their coastal bases in relays. In anticipation of such a coup, the RAF had developed a plan based around torpedo-launching Swordfish biplanes.

Franz Fiby of 3./JG 2 recalled:

> We were airborne at 11:45 from Calais-Marck with 16 aircraft. My Schwarm was to furnish cover on the land side of the convoy. We caught sight of our ships off Boulogne and escorted them as far as Cap Gris-Nez where we were relieved by Fw 190s. At that time the ships were still undetected by the British so we saw no action. The sortie was hard work—high levels of concentration had to be maintained in very gloomy visibility some 200 meters below the cloud deck and in total radio silence. We landed back at Calais-Marck after an hour's flying time and had lunch. From the airfield we could hear the booming of the coastal batteries as they opened up … the 16 of us then went back to cockpit readiness. From the ground we caught brief glimpses of a dogfight going on overhead.

The Fleet Air Arm's response—Operation *Fuller*—condemned the crews of the Swordfish torpedo bombers to almost certain death. They had the misfortune to reach the convoy and launch their attack in the precise sector where JG 26's and JG 2's fighter coverage converged. Banks of cloud and fog could offer little protection when setting up for a straight run-in against the ships. Out of the ensuing hail of withering fire and the confusion of battle that

Oblt. Siegfried Bethke's 2./JG 2 Bf 109 F-4 Black 1. Note ten victory markings at the top of the rudder. Staffelkapitän Bethke had returned his tenth victory the previous summer, on July 24, 1941. Seen in Haamstede in the Netherlands following a sortie during the *Donnerkeil* operation, February 1942, in Siberian-like conditions.

Fw 190 A Red 12 of 2./JG 26 assigned to Lt. Gottfried Dietze, at Arques-Saint-Omer, early 1942.

blasted all six Swordfish out of the air, II./JG 2 eventually claimed and was credited with no fewer than eight Swordfish, while III./JG 26 claimed three and the ships' anti-aircraft batteries were credited with a further four. Lt. Graf von Einsiedel was credited with two Swordfish shot down:

> We had just overflown the *Scharnhorst* when I sighted six torpedo bombers on my port side which we identified as Swordfish types. They were flying in two formations, a group of four and two together on their own. The crews did not appear particularly experienced; they were making no evasive maneuvers. I focused on the first formation, ploughing along at no more than 110 kph, their fixed undercarriage barely cresting the tops of the waves.

In total JG 2 filed some 17 claims for February 12 and, unlike JG 26, sustained no losses. A Spitfire brought down by Staffelkapitän "Assi" Hahn was his 50th victory. III./JG 2 claimed Whirlwinds of 137 Sqn shot down. Two Hampdens and two Blenheims from a late-afternoon raid mounted by some 70 RAF Bomber Command machines were also claimed by JG 2, one of the last actions of the Geschwader before cover duties were taken over by JG 1 based in the Netherlands.

After this spectacular operation, tensions subsided. The RAF continued its intrusions on the continent but on a smaller scale. Even if Ultra kept the Allies informed, fighters and bombers found themselves facing the guns of the German fighters who were constantly winning victories. In one three-day period between April 14 and 17, 1942 7./JG 2 claimed no fewer than 17 victories including eight for Staffelkapitän Oblt. Egon Mayer. This included two Spitfires on 16 April for his 31st and 32nd victories and three more the following day (two unconfirmed). By day on April 17, 1942, the RAF sent out a small force of Lancasters

Lt. Egon Mayer climbing into the cockpit of his Bf 109 Friedrich White 1. As the Staffelführer of 7./JG 2—note the metal pennant on the aerial mast and the 7. Staffel *Zylinderhut* "top hat" emblem—Lt. Egon Mayer was awarded the Knight's Cross on August 1, 1941.

Lt. Jakob Augustin of 7./JG 2 flew White 8 (W.Nr. 333) and returned his 12th victory on June 6, 1942.

over the Continent—a low-level raiding force to attack the MAN diesel engine works at Augsburg, deep in Bavaria. Fw. Otto Pohl of 5./JG 2 registered the Geschwader's 1,000th combat success with the downing of one bomber.

Mayer's last victory with the Bf 109 was a claim for a Spitfire shot down on May 7, 1942. At that point Staffelkapitän Mayer and his 7. Staffel were taken off operations to convert onto the new Fw 190 fighter. Conversion training took place in Théville. Within a month, 7. Staffel was back in action. The first clash of III./JG 2's new Fw 190s and RAF Spitfires took place on June 3, 1942 in a hard-fought action north of Cherbourg. In a letter home, 7./JG 2 pilot Uffz. Otto Kleinert wrote:

> On one of my first sorties from Théville with 7./JG 2 on June 3 we ran into a formation of about ten Spitfires and shot them all down—our Focke-Wulfs are largely superior to their machines. I flew as Lt. Augustin's wingman but really saw very little of the action, so close did I stick to my leader's rudder. After we landed I was somewhat surprised to learn that we had accounted for so many enemy machines. Of course as a relative beginner I had little appreciation of the bigger picture.

403 Sqn (Royal Canadian Air Force) lost at least seven Spitfires in this action with Mayer himself claiming two, his 43rd and 44th victories. Among the other 7./JG 2 aces Ofw. Willi Stratmann, Uffz. Guenther Toll and Lt. Jakob Augustin all returned victories. Obfw. Alfred Knies returned his first victory, which was feted as the 100th for the Staffel. The next day 7. Staffel was again in action against RAF Spitfires claiming four more, and on 6 June Knies returned his second victory, another Spitfire. JG filed some 23 claims for Spitfires on this date alone.

The intensity of the fighting along the Channel and the transfer of a number of JG 2 veterans to Geschwader engaged in fighting on the Eastern Front saw the Richthofen receive a

Oblt. Egon Mayer, about to climb down from the controls of a Stab III./JG 2 Friedrich, seen relating a successful combat account to his chief mechanic, Gefr. Bender, around April 17, 1942. Mayer's eight claims in three days during April included two Spitfires on April 16 for his 31st and 32nd victories.

Mayer returned his 49th victory on August 19, 1942 and his 50th the following day. A member of JG 2 since the fall of 1939, Mayer was appointed Gruppenkommandeur of III./JG 2 in November 1942 and is credited with developing the "head-on" method of attacking bombers.

number of reinforcements during June. One of the most notable departures to the East was 5./JG 2's Fw. Otto Pohl and Wolfgang Wehrhagen of 4./JG 2. Both pilots went to JG 77 while a third, Kurt Rose, was posted to JG 51—of these three pilots only Pohl survived the war. Several JG 77 pilots were posted back to the Channel Front with JG 2—among them Lt. Bruno Siekmann who had achieved ten victories in a year of fighting in the East with II./JG 77. Lt. Hermann Staege—a champion in the pre-war Kunstflugstaffel aerobatics team, incorporated into I./LG 2 during 1939/40, a Gruppe that had been redesignated I./JG 77—also returned to the West with JG 2. He was credited with 15 victories at the time of his transfer. As most of these Eastern Front veterans were Bf 109 pilots, they too underwent the Fw 190 conversion before joining JG 2.

On July 21, 1942 Hptm. Helmut-Felix Bolz, Kommandeur of II./JG 2, shot down an unknown aircraft type that he initially identified as a "Tomahawk." A short while later he visited the crash site at Caudebec-en-Caux between Rouen and Le Havre and was able to inspect at first hand what he later learned was a P-51 Mustang. The pilot, Flt. Lt. Veal Rowland of 239 Squadron had been taken captive.

In 1942 the overwhelming majority of Knight's Crosses were awarded to pilots fighting in the East. One exception was Maj. Johannes Seifert, leading I. /JG 26, who received the Knight's Cross for his 36 *Luftsiege* on August 12.

Losses among the ranks of the Luftwaffe aces in the West were steady but limited. The Kommandeur of I./JG 2, Hptm. Ignatz Prestele, was shot down on May 4, 1942 in combat with Spitfires off Cape Antifer at the controls of Bf 109 F-4 (W.Nr. 8404). Appointed Kommandeur of I./JG 2 on November 21, 1941 this 20-victory ace had previously

On August 12, 1942, Maj. Johannes Seifert (I./JG 26) was called to Marshal Hugo Sperrle's Paris headquarters to receive the Knight's Cross, a ceremony covered by the Luftwaffe magazine *Der Adler*.

JG 2 ace "Sepp" Wurmheller's Fw 190 at readiness.

been Staffelkapitän 2./JG 53 during the Battle of Britain, returning his 7th and 8th victories on September 29, 1940. His 9th was not achieved until the opening day of *Barbarossa*. On July 31, 1942, Oblt. Rudolf Pflanz, leading 11./JG 2 (52 victories) and a Knight's Cross bearer, was killed near Dieppe.

At that time, the dispersion of the JGs in the West was still along "classic" lines. JG 1 was divided between the Netherlands (Woendsrecht/Bergen-op-Zoom) and northern Germany; JG 2 was dispersed between Beaumont and Caen, while JG 26 was based principally in France (Saint-Omer/Abbeville) with a detachment in Belgium (Wevelgem). Fw 190s equipped a single Gruppe in JG 1 but made up 90 percent of the other two Geschwader.

The second major engagement in the West during 1942 occurred over Dieppe. Faced with the launch of *Fall Blau*, Stalin demanded the immediate opening of a second front. An Allied landing in 1942 was nevertheless unthinkable; however, to satisfy Stalin, Churchill authorized Operation *Jubilee*, an air/sea attack targeting only the limited area of Dieppe. The result was disaster. By the end of the day on August 19, 106 Allied aircraft had been lost against some 58 German aircraft. Underlining the determination of the German fighter pilot was one particular performance: Ofw. Josef Wurmheller (1./JG 2) had had a "domestic" accident a few days earlier and flew his sorties with his foot in a cast. Despite this handicap, "Sepp" Wurmheller clambered into his Fw 190 A-3, took off and shot down two Spitfires for his 54th and 55th victories (timed at 09:08 and 09:12). Shortly afterward, victim of a Boston's defensive fire, he had to force-land his Fw 190 near Dieppe but got away with some bruising and compressed vertebrae. In similar fashion, Ofw. Günther Seeger force-landed his Fw 190 A-3 after returning his 20th and 21st. Both quickly returned to Triqueville and to the fray. By the end of the day, Wurmheller had accounted for seven opponents. The feat earned him a promotion for bravery (*Tapferkeitsoffizier*) to the rank of Leutnant and the award of the

Heinz Klems (right) of the Stab I./JG 26 received the Iron Cross 2nd class on August 14, 1942 for his first victory, a Spitfire shot down near Etaples on July 31. At left are Oblt. Hösl, and Lt. Hans Dippel (behind Hösl). Klems would fly only his tenth combat sortie five days later—over Dieppe.

"*Nach einem Einsatz gegen ein Britisches Landungsunternehmen.*" Returning from combat over Dieppe, 7./JG 2 pilots Holzapfel and Stratmann are seen with Kommandeur Hahn (right) on August 19, 1942. Stratmann downed a Spitfire, two kilometres west of Dieppe at 16:10 for his 12th victory.

German Cross in Gold, presented on August 21, 1942 with his score around 60 victories. The German Cross in Gold usually preceded the award of the Knight's Cross but Wurmheller had already worn this decoration for nearly a year.

However, this Allied defeat had not erased the unpleasant surprise experienced by the *Jagdflieger* two days previously. On August 17, the USAAF—starting to arrive in numbers on English soil—launched its first attack on France, targeting Rouen-Sotteville station. B-17 Fortresses flew in "boxes," concentrations of four-engine aircraft from which machine-gunners could cover each other. (This was not the German fighter pilots' first encounter with this four-engine aircraft, since in August 1941, an RAF B-17 had already been shot down by JG 2.) Jules Meimberg's 11./JG 2 based at Saint-Pol countered the raid. His Staffel had taken charge of 15 examples of the latest Bf 109 fighter just a few months previously—the Gustav G-1 with a pressurized cockpit to counter the threat of British reconnaissance machines operating at high altitude.

> We were climbing westwards out over the coast in brilliant sunshine when suddenly out over the glittering sea I saw a sight that left me rubbing my eyes in amazement: a good dozen or so four-engine bombers flying in close and perfect formation heading south. With the sun at our backs the escorts had not spotted us. We threw our kites into a steep dive and closed on the *Viermots* from astern at high speed. I calmly picked out a target. Suddenly, with an almighty *bang!* all hell broke loose. My Messerschmitt seemed to have been caught in a web of tracers

Lt. Kurt Bühligen climbing down from his Fw 190 after a sortie over the beaches at Dieppe. He was credited with four kills on August 19, 1942, as was Oblt. Siegfried Schnell of 9./JG 2 (67–70).

Josef "Sepp" Wurmheller (center) achieved 102 kills over 300 missions. He was killed in action over Alençon, France on June 22, 1944.

> and every man in that formation seemed to have a heavy machine gun and was unleashing salvo upon salvo at one target—myself and my kite. The silhouette of the bomber grew slowly—painfully slowly—ever larger in my gunsight. "Closer … don't mess this up! Now it's filled the entire sight. Open fire!" And then, "Pull up! " But I had been deceived by the huge wingspan of the behemoth—my rounds fell hopelessly short of the target.

Meimberg had encountered the 12 B-17s of the 97th Bombardment Group (BG) led by Paul Tibbets—later to drop the atomic bomb on Hiroshima. The Germans quickly grew to appreciate that the American four-engine bombers—*Viermots*—with their heavy defensive armament and well able to absorb punishment especially when flying in their mutually protective "combat boxes," were tough opponents. Operating close to the limits of the high-altitude performance of the Bf 109 and Fw 190 fighters, their 40-meter wingspans filled the fighter's gun sights while they were still some way out of range.

Meimberg recalled:

> We sought out as much information on these machines as we could find … first flight in 1935, steadily upgraded and improved … three revolving turrets, eight heavy machine guns for defense … and only one point of weakness—the cockpit. Whereas Mayer wanted to launch attacks from all directions simultaneously to disperse the defensive fire, I argued that head-on—hitting the B-17s where their defensive fire was at its weakest—was the only certain way to bring a Fortress down. [The B-17 F had only one forward-firing 0.50 cal with a poor field of fire.]

American airmen, confident in their heavy bombers, were increasingly committing over the Continent, gradually replacing the RAF in its daytime attacks. It was not until September 6 that, during a raid on Drucat, Longuenesse, and Méaulte, the Tagjagd claimed six B-17s. Even if these six *Viermot* claims were actually reduced to two, these were the first USAAF B-17s downed in combat by German fighters.

Many of the U.S. Eighth Air Force's early raids on Continental Europe were launched against U-boat pens. Saint-Nazaire was raided on 23 November by 36 bombers including eight B-24s. Gradually, the USAAF embarked on its first operations over the Reich. From August 17 to December 31, of the 747 B-17s

Julius Meimberg Staffelkapitän 11./JG 2, relaxes next to his Bf 109 G-1 White 11.

Uffz. Friedrich May of 8./JG 2 (sitting left) killing time between sorties with a game of chess alongside Black 13. May returned his first victory on June 10, 1942 when he claimed a Boston at 14:10. His victim was AL283 of 107 Sqn. His first B-17 claim was filed after the November 23 raid on Saint-Nazaire. He was killed on October 20, 1943 in the vicinity of Rouen in combat with Spitfires (Fw 190 A-6 470047) as an Ofw. with 3./JG 2. With at least 21 kills to his name, May was awarded a posthumous German Cross in Gold.

engaged in 26 operations, only 31 of them were lost (4.2 percent). This low rate is explained by the proximity of targets allowing the presence of a fighter escort. Escort to distant objectives was out of the question for these early raids and with fighters enjoying limited autonomy, the Fortresses had to prove their effectiveness. While awaiting this threat, fighting continued over northern France. Lt. Wurmheller was awarded the Oak Leaves on November 13, 1942 for 60 *Abschüsse*.

New pilots arrived at 7./JG 2. Lt. Georg-Peter Eder was a 12-victory ace who had spent the previous year at Jagdfliegerschule 2. Eder flew into Beaumont-le Roger to meet Oesau several days after the 23 November raid.

> I learnt that I was posted to 7. Staffel in Vannes commanded by my old friend Erich Hohagen. The next morning I "discovered" the Fw 190 and spent virtually the entire day in the air getting to grips with the controls and exploring its performance. We flew a number of different types of formation exercise, always pushing the aircraft to its limits. 7. Staffel was a unit mostly composed of aces with scores that largely exceeded those of the other Staffeln. It wasn't easy to integrate.

One of the last actions of 1942 on the Channel Front was the U.S. Eight Air Force raid on the U-boat pens at Lorient on December 30, 1942—the 27th mission of this fledgling force flown by 40 B-17s. JG 2 Kommandeur Mayer and his Stab along with nine Fw 190s from 7. Staffel were airborne from Vannes to counter the incursion. Mayer was determined to try a new tactic that he had been considering over the previous weeks—the frontal attack, hitting the B-17s where their defensive fire was at its weakest. In the subsequent fight Lt. Eder returned his first *Viermot* victory in his first encounter with the four-engine bombers:

> today the fine weather—absent since Christmas—put in a welcome reappearance. The comrades from the other side were bound to take advantage to make their last visit of the year. At around 10:00 we were informed that bombers were forming up over England and by 10:30 they had set out on a southwesterly heading. The order quickly came through to go to cockpit readiness and we waited for the order to get airborne which could reach us at any moment.

Scoreboard of 7./JG 2 for 1941 and 1942—the majority of the kills were made out over the sea.

Once in the air the Kommandeur set course for Lorient and we climbed for altitude in wide circles. A constant stream of detail regarding the position of the enemy aircraft came over the radio. They were approaching Lorient from the sea. Then we saw the swarms far off in the distance. The Kommandeur called over the radio: "Tighten up the formation, stay calm, we are attacking from the front." As we closed up, the enemy formation grew rapidly larger. The Kommandeur took us into a slight turn to bring us in head-on. Gunsights were switched on and cannon electrically cocked. "Stay calm, do not open fire," the voice of the Kommandeur came through the headphones. By now the bombers were looming large in the windshield.

"Now!"

There was just time to unleash a burst of fire before sweeping over a B-17 and then a steeply banked turn to come in from the rear. All over my machine I could hear cracking and popping but I clung on to my prey, closing to within 150 meters. His port inboard engine was already ablaze but he maintained his position in the formation. Hundreds of tracer rounds seemed to be drawn to my canopy. My fire was unceasing. By now the Fortress was burning from one end to the other. Then in an instant it appeared to tip over and started going down, plunging some 8,000 meters into the Atlantic. No time for a breather, the bombers were approaching their target. Bombs gone! They appeared to fall harmlessly into the ocean. As the B-17s headed back out to sea we continued to harass them—like flies buzzing around a large beast. And we knew where to bite. Then another hit in my port wing—I could see that this one had caused some damage. Off to my right I could see Erich Hohagen firing burst after burst and taking hits that did not appear to bother him in the slightest. The Kommandeur ordered us to reassemble over Belle Ile and in a matter of minutes we were back over Vannes where we landed on our last drops of fuel. As I taxied back to the 7. Staffel dispersal I saw the Fw 190 of Lt. Philipp—the Adjutant—alongside mine. It was in a sorry state, riddled from front to back. In the cockpit a beaming Philipp waved at me, a broad grin on his face. Back in the ops room we animatedly discussed the battle, each successful pilot writing up his victory report and checking for witnesses. Eight bombers downed for two pilots missing.

"For our first formation frontal attack that was a good result," declared the Kommandeur.

Lt. Georg-Peter Eder of 7./JG 2 (petting the dogs), and the new Staffelkapitän of 7./JG 2, Oblt. Eric Hohagen (at left), who had returned 31 victories with JG 51 prior to sustaining serious injuries on September 7, 1941.

Bf 109 F-4 Black 2 flown by Lt. Lothar Myrrhe of 5./JG 3, on Sicily, during the spring of 1942. Myrrhe returned around 18 victories but was reported missing on April 21, 1943 in the East.

The Mediterranean, 1942

In 1942, the deployment of the Tagjagd in the southern sector was very different from that of 1941. First, the British winter offensive led to the urgent transfer of II./JG 3 to Sicily to help neutralize Malta. This Gruppe was subordinated to JG 53, fully engaged at that time in the Mediterranean. Shuttling between Sicily and Africa, to support JG 27, its pilots often carried out escorts or *Jabo* missions, balancing losses and victories.

The Kommandeur, Hptm. Karl-Heinz Krahl, was killed by anti-aircraft fire over Malta. Krahl, a former bomber pilot in Spain, led I./JG 2 in 1940, won the Knight's Cross and had returned 24 victories. Shortly afterward, II./JG 3 returned to the Eastern Front for the summer offensive.

JG 27, taken over in June by Oberstleutnant "Edu" Neumann, continued to compete for mastery of the skies with the Desert Air Force. On February 22, Oblt. Marseille was finally rewarded with the Knight's Cross for his 50 victories. Further awards were not long in coming: the Oak Leaves on June 6 for 75 victories, the Swords on June 18 for 101 victories and the Diamonds on September 3 for 126 *Abschüsse*. But, once again, this plethora of

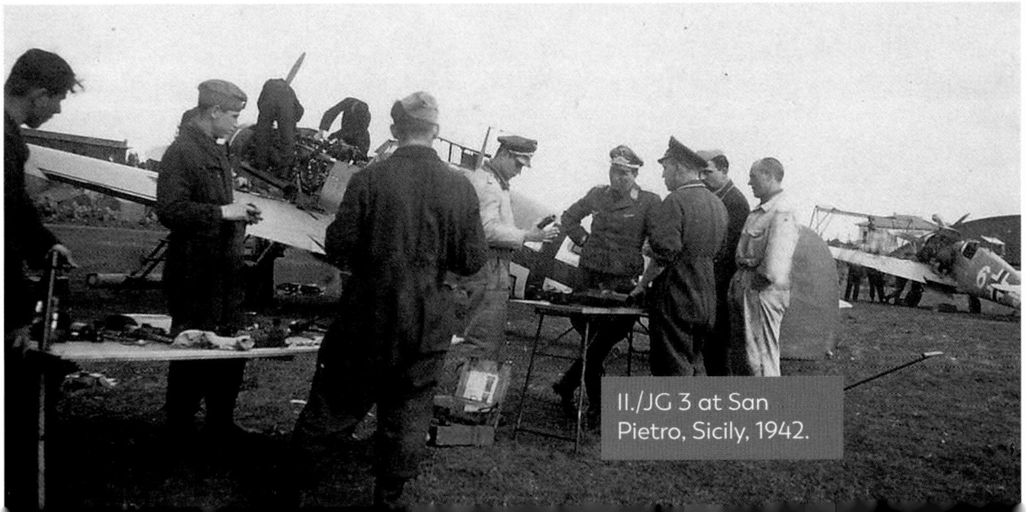

II./JG 3 at San Pietro, Sicily, 1942.

A Bf 109 F of the Stab II./JG 3. Flugzeugführer Gefr. Arnold Bringmann is seen returning after achieving a kill on July 1, 1942. Bringmann had 28 confirmed claims, 24 in Russia (plus two unconfirmed) and four in the West (plus one unconfirmed B-17).

successes did not come easily. Despite the exotic life in Africa, fatigue was keenly felt. The last photos of Marseille show him largely exhausted by tension and loss. Comradeship was no empty word in the desert and Marseille was affected by the loss of so many of his comrades. The hardest was that of Oblt. Hans-Arnold Stahlschmidt who disappeared in the sands on September 7, 1942 (in January 1944, he would receive the Knight's Cross posthumously for his 60 victories).

"Fifi" Stahlschmidt was not the only ace to die in North Africa. On June 17, 1942, the Pomeranian Oblt. Otto Schulz (4./JG 27) went missing near Sidi Rezegh after shooting down a P-40, his 51st victory. He had been awarded the Knight's Cross for his 50th victory. Oblt. Fritz Körner (2./JG 27) was shot down by Hurricanes on July 4, 1942 near El Alamein. He entered captivity but in September was awarded the Knight's Cross for his 36 victories.

For its part, JG 53 "Pik As" (Ace of Spades) was heavily committed from Sicily against Malta while some operations were mounted on the African continent later in the year in support of JG 27. Bomber escorts, *Jabo* missions, free hunts, ground strafing, shipping attacks, search for airmen at sea, protection of the Seenot seaplanes … the fighter pilots of JG 53 quickly became "all-rounders." As a result, JG 53 distinguished itself, but long sorties over water led to an increase in pilot losses.

April 1942 saw the high point of raids on Malta: JG 53 flew some 4,300 sorties over the island of which only 1,400 were free-hunt sorties. Throughout the month all three Gruppen of JG 53 flew as a rule two daily sorties over the island, although individual pilots could fly a third or a fourth. Mission orders were usually as escort for bombers or fighter-bombers as well as free hunts. Strafing sorties against Maltese airfields were also flown toward the end of the month.

Contact with the enemy increased from April 20 with the arrival of 46 Spitfires on the island brought in on the U.S. carrier *Wasp*, following a first delivery on March 7. The first Spitfire shot down over Malta was claimed on March 10 by Uffz. Hans Schade of 8./JG 53 for his 13th victory. Schade was reported missing after a clash with

"Jochen" Marseille in the cockpit of his famous Bf 109 Yellow 14.

Marseille, with a clutch of ground crew, in his equally well-known Kübelwagen *Otto* (8 in Italian) commemorating eight of his victories obtained in record time.

Spitfires over Grand Harbour on April 1. On this date Kommodore von Maltzahn returned his 60th kill and Oblt. Helmut Belser of 8./JG 53 his twentieth. Elsewhere Kommandeur III./JG 53 Wilcke had 35 and Oblt. Michalski of 4./JG 53 had 29 kills. Lt. Herbert Schramm of 8./JG 53 was already a Knight's Cross holder but was posted to a training school early in the month. On April 2 Kommandeur Spies II./JG 53 claimed a Spitfire for his third. On April 10, Staffelführer 6./JG 53 Lt. Hermann Neuhoff was shot down by a Hurricane (but may have fallen to a Bf 109) and taken captive. He was subsequently awarded the Knight's Cross for his 40 victories (23 in the East).

At the end of April, III./JG 53 was transferred to North Africa, where Oblt. Helmut Belser, Staffelkapitän 8./JG 53, was killed in a takeoff accident at Castel Benito on June 19. Leaving II./JG 53 to continue operations over Malta, I./JG 53 returned to the East before returning to Sicily in October 1942. Elements of the unit flew into Tobruk on October 30 but left their aircraft behind for JG 27 on returning to Sicily in mid-November. On November 25, the Gruppenstab and 1. and 2. Staffeln flew to Djedeida, some 30 kilometers west of Tunis, while 3./JG 53 remained on Sicily and flew escort for shipping bringing in supplies to Tunisia. In December—after the rains—sorties were flown from Bizerte including at least one interception of 18 B-17s raiding the port. During this period Julius Meimberg's 11./JG 2 was subordinated to the Gruppe.

In mid 1942, I./JG 77 was withdrawn from the Eastern Front to support actions against Malta. Flying from Sicily the Kapitän of 1./JG 77, Oblt. Siegfried Freytag, was in the thick of the fighting. On September 15, 1./JG 77 claimed three Spitfires. On 17 September Oblt.

Although not showing the Ace of Spades, this Bf 109 F with auxiliary tank in Sicily is a III./JG 53 machine.

A Bf 109 F-4 of 4./JG 53 in the spring of 1942 at Comiso. Note the two-color segmented upper-surface camouflage scheme.

Maj. Günther. von Maltzahn (left) and his wingman in front of a Geschwaderstab Friedrich in its protective "box" at Comiso, Sicily, 1942. The aircraft has gun cameras in both wings so is likely to have been flown by the "boss."

Oblt. Otto Böhner, Staffelkapitän of 6./JG 53, seen on his return from a sortie over Malta during early 1942. He was wounded by anti-aircraft fire over Malta on March 7 but was able to land safely back in Comiso. He was replaced by 36-victory ace Lt. Hermann Neuhoff, who was named Staffelführer.

A Sicilian airfield, possibly Gela, 1942. Hptm. Herbert Kaminski, a little-known Knight's Cross bearer, was appointed Gruppenkommandeur I./JG 53 after Von Werra's death on October 25, 1941 and is seen here (center) after returning from a sortie—his Bf 109 F-4 with its wide white fuselage band is in the background. He was badly injured in a landing accident on July 24, 1942 owing to engine failure. After convalescence he returned to combat and survived the war.

Freytag shot down another Spitfire on a free hunt but I./JG 77 lost its first Bf 109 Gustav. The pilot, Uffz. Friedrich Schneider, recalled:

> In the summer of 1942, I arrived at 3./JG 77 then based in Comiso. My Staffelkapitän was Oblt. Friedrich Geisshardt. On September 17, we were returning from a mission, flying at 6,000 meters. My Kapitän and I entered a shallow dive to check that the airspace below was "clean." Banking into a hard turn to port to rejoin the formation, Geisshardt shouted at me over the radio: "Schneider, climb!" I shot a glance over my shoulder—two Spitfires behind me at about 50 meters, in a shooting position. I pulled up my machine and let it slide to the left.

A 126 Sqn Spitfire opened up with a five-second burst. The right side of Schneider's Bf 109 G-2 was hit, injuring him in the foot. With difficulty he extricated himself from the cockpit and jumped clear.

> I found myself swinging under my parachute and the Spitfires were circling around me. They were waggling their wings, so I waved at them. After several minutes, I hit the water, to the northeast of Malta. I got rid of the parachute. My lifejacket was full of shrapnel. I unhooked the life raft and tugged the inflation handle. I had three goes at hauling myself up into the dinghy. Far above me, I could see my comrades. Obviously, they hadn't spotted me, so I wouldn't be able to count on one of our sea rescue machines coming to my rescue. After a long wait, the silhouette

Just arrived in Sicily from the East, Lt. Armin Köhler of 3./JG 77 shows off his scoreboard to his Italian comrades. Köhler survived the war, having achieved around 40 victories and been awarded the Knight's Cross.

Staffelkapitän 3./JG 77 Oblt. Friedrich Geisshardt (left) was awarded the Oak Leaves in June 1942. Here he is seen at Gela, Sicily, with Günther von Maltzahn (JG 53) and Heinz Bär (I./JG 77), also wearing their Oak Leaves awards.

> of an English rescue launch loomed into view … Two men hoisted me onto a narrow bridge. Disembarked at the port of Valletta, English soldiers had to protect me from Maltese civilians who attempted to molest me. I was taken to hospital.

After three months of detention with about 20 German airmen, Schneider was loaded on a cruiser and ended the war in a prison camp in Egypt. He returned to Germany in 1947.

On 30 September 1942, "Jochen" Marseille was killed bailing out of a Bf 109 G. The death of Marseille coincided with a very different new phase in aerial warfare over Africa. As it happened, on October 23, the Allies launched a decisive offensive at El Alamein. The situation could probably have been saved once again if the Anglo-Americans had not landed in Morocco and Algeria. Decimated by the constant fighting, JG 27 was withdrawn from this theater of operations and then dispersed.

II. and III./JG 77 arrived urgently from the East to compensate for the departure of Neumann's Geschwader while I./JG 77 moved from Sicily to Africa. II./JG 51, temporarily refitting in Germany, was also sent to Tunisia as well as the Bf 109s of JG 2. The situation was delicate because the Germans would find, in addition to new American opponents, more sophisticated machines in the air: USAAF P-38 Lightnings and RAF Spitfires had finally reached African skies.

One of the first aces lost was Hptm. Wolf-Dieter Huy, leading 7./JG 77. He had immediately noted the difference in the fighting: "In the USSR, we flew very low in small units; in Africa, we operated at very high altitude with powerful formations." Shot down by Spitfires near El Alamein on 28 October 1942, this 40-year-old *Experte* entered captivity.

Covering the Via Balbia, JG 77 aided the remnants of the Axis troops withdrawing into the Tunisian redoubt where they were to fight their last battles.

JG 27 departed Africa in November 1942, the end of a "beautiful period" for the Austrian Oblt. Rudolf Sinner of 6./JG 27 (flanked here by his two mechanics). An excellent pilot, Rudi Sinner achieved 39 victories and survived the war.

Afterword

The emphasis on victories, honors and promotions in this account is typical of the Luftwaffe frontline fighter units. German fighter pilots had an almost overriding concern for the *Abschussliste*. With the launch of *Barbarossa* in June 1941, many *Jagdflieger* were able to run up colossal scores.

Lt. Johann Badum was typical of the young fighter pilots arriving on the Eastern Front. Born in Ruthweiler, a municipality in Rhineland-Pfalz, he joined JG 77 in 1941 aged 20. In January 1942, Badum was serving in the advanced training wing of JG 77—the Ergängzungsstaffel. On February 26, 1942 he claimed a Pe-2 bomber for his first victory. In April 1942 he transferred to 6. Staffel of JG 77, with three victories in 45 missions by this time. He saw combat over Sevastopol during June 1942—his 9th claim with 6./JG 77 was a Yak-1 on June 3. He claimed a further 17 victories in July 1942 to raise his total to twenty-nine. On August 6, 1942, he was airborne from Kastornoye, Ukraine, after being scrambled following the appearance of a single Russian reconnaissance aircraft. That same day he wrote to his parents:

> This morning I achieved my 30th kill—that sounds better than 29. For me it was the first contact with the enemy in almost 14 days. And it was just a single bomber, one of the most modern, a Pe-2, which of course was "had for breakfast." Nevertheless, I haven't been awarded the German Cross, because now 35 victories are required. There was a time when there used to be a Knight's Cross for 20 under normal circumstances. If there was anything more going on, I would still hope to get it, but with such lean pickings here, I won't be getting a sausage. Every fortnight there's one downing, I won't get it that way. If the Russians don't have the friendly consideration to launch a counteroffensive, then I'll be left completely high and dry.

Badum achieved his ambition—he was awarded the Knight's Cross on October 15,

Johann Badum (March 2, 1921–January 12, 1943) was shot down and killed in combat with USAAF P-38 fighters over Libya.

A yellow-nosed JG 77 Bf 109 during the summer of 1942 in the Ukraine. Note the tarps protecting the tires from the sun.

1942 after 51 victories. Shortly thereafter he went to North Africa with II./JG 77 and was appointed Staffelkapitän 6./JG 77. He claimed two P-40s shot down on December 21, 1942 for his 52nd and 53rd victories. On January 12, 1943 he was airborne at the controls of Bf 109 G-2 (W.Nr. 10727) Yellow 7 to counter a 97th BG B-17 raid on Castel Benito airfield. Caught up in a clash with American P-38s, he was shot down and killed. He had been awarded the Iron Cross 1st and 2nd Class, the Luftwaffe Honor Cup and the German Cross in Gold, the usual precursor to the Knight's Cross. Badum achieved his victories during the course of some 300 missions; his total included 14 IL-2 Sturmoviks.

Badum's death in Africa provided a foretaste of what was to come for the *Jagdflieger*. It was the Allied bomber fleets that would write down the Wehrmacht on the ground. In many theaters the *Jagdflieger* would be hard pushed to take on the bombers effectively. New weapons and tactics had to be tried and tested and new units hurriedly established, while all the time losses grew alarmingly. Violent death was never far away.

Glossary

Abschuss	a kill, a downing (pl. *Abschüsse*)
Bereitschaft	readiness
BG	Bombardment Group (USAAF)
Einsatz	operational mission (pl. *Einsätze*)
Experte	ace (pl. *Experten*)
Feindberührung	contact with the enemy
Feindflug	a flight over enemy territory (pl. *Feindflüge*)
Fhr.	Fähnrich (Fahnenjunker)/Flight Officer
Flugplatz	airfield (pl. *Flugplätze*)
Frontflug	a sortie, combat sortie
Frontflugspange	operational missions clasp awarded to frontline pilots with a specified number of sorties
Fw.	Feldwebel/Technical Sergeant
Gefr.	Gefreiter/Aircraftman/Airman
Geschwader	a wing/group, comprising 90–120 aircraft (pl. Geschwader)
Gruppe	autonomous Luftwaffe group, smaller than a USAAF group/RAF wing but larger than a squadron (pl. Gruppen)
Hptm.	Hauptmann/Captain/Flight Lieutenant
Jabo	dive-bomber, or fighter-bomber
Jagdflieger	fighter pilot
Jagdgeschwader	a fighter wing/group, comprising 90–120 aircraft (abbr. JG)
Jagdgruppe	a fighter group (abbr. JGr.)
Lt.	Leutnant/Second Lieutenant/Pilot Officer
Luftsieg	air victory (pl. *Luftsiege*)
Maj.	Major/Squadron Leader
Obfw.	Oberfeldwebel/Flight Sergeant/Master Sergeant
Oblt.	Oberleutnant/First Lieutenant/Flying Officer
P.O.	Pilot Officer
Richthofen	JG 2, named after Manfred von Richthofen
Rotte	a pair of aircraft, lit. pack (pl. Rotten)
RVT	Reichsverteidigung, air defense of the Reich
Schlageter	JG 26, named after Albert Leo Schlageter
Schwarm	a flight, lit. a swarm, comprising 4–6 aircraft (pl. Schwärme)
Sitzbereitschaft	cockpit readiness
Sqn	Squadron
Stab	Staff Flight
Staffel	a flight squadron/echelon comprising 9–12 aircraft (pl. Staffeln)
Tagjagd	day fighter arm of the WWII Luftwaffe
Tagjäger	day fighters
Uffz.	Unteroffizier/Corporal (RAF)/Sergeant (USAAF)
Ufw.	Unterfeldwebel/Sergeant
W.Nr.	*Werk Nummer*, factory number (of an aircraft)

Bibliography

Aders, G., *Jagdgeschwader 51 Mölders* (Motorbuch, 1999)

Eriksson, P., *Alarmstart East* (Amberley, 2017)

Johnston, D., *German Eagles in Spanish Skies* (Schiffer, 2019)

Mombeeck, Erik, *Jagdgeschwader 2: In the Skies of France* (Vol. I: Porte d'Hoves, self-published, trans. Neil Page)

__________, *Jagdgeschwader 26: The Abbeville Boys* (Luftwaffe Gallery unit Special: Porte d'Hoves, self-published, trans. Neil Page)

__________, *Jagdgeschwader 5: Fighters of the Midnight Sun* (Luftwaffe Gallery unit Special: Porte d'Hoves, self-published, trans. Neil Page)

__________, *Jagdgeschwader 54: The Green Hearts* (Luftwaffe Gallery Unit Special: Porte d'Hoves, self-published, trans. Neil Page)

__________, *Jagdgeschwader 77: Fighting on All Fronts* (Luftwaffe Gallery Unit Special: Porte d'Hoves, self-published, trans. Neil Page)

Obermaier, E., *Die Ritterkreuzträger der Luftwaffe* (Verlag Dieter Hoffmann)

Page, Neil, *Aircraft in Profile: Focke Wulf 190 A* (Scale Aircraft Modelling, November 2002)

Prien, J., *Die Jagdfliegerverbände der Deutschen Luftwaffe* (purple series) (Struve Druck/Rogge, multiple volumes)

__________, *Geschichte des Jagdgeschwader 77* (Struve Druck, 4 vols)

Roba, Jean-Louis, *Les As de la chasse de Jour allemande, 1939–1945* (ETAI, 2012)

__________, *The Luftwaffe in Africa* (Casemate Illustrated, 2019)

Rodeike, P., *Focke Wulf Jagdflugzeug 190* (Struve Druck, Eutin 1998. ISBN 3-923 457-44-8: German text)

Stipdonk, P., *Das Jagdgeschwader 51 Mölders* (VDM, 1996)

Timin, Mikhail, *Air Battles over the Baltic, 1941* (Helion, 2018)

Index